Confronting Your Mountains

By

Jennifer Alexander
&
Anu Nicholas

Psalms 139:7-12 (NIV)

"Where can I go from your Spirit? Where can I flee from your presence? If I go up to the heavens, you are there; if I make my bed in the depths, you are there. If I rise on the wings of the dawn, if I settle on the far side of the sea, even there your hand will guide me, your right hand will hold me fast. If I say, "Surely the darkness will hide me and the light become night around me," even the darkness will not be dark to you; the night will shine like the day, for darkness is as light to you."

Acknowledgment

It's always for God.

Working together with Anu was so wonderful; we both acknowledge it is the heavenly Father who filled our hearts with His inspiration. We are encouraged by the wonderful work that God is doing in us to draw men unto Him. We also would like to thank everyone who motivated us. There are so many names to mention here, and we are ever thankful for the lovely people in our lives. Glory to God in the Highest!

1 Thessalonians 5:11 (NIV)

"Therefore encourage one another and build each other up, just as you are doing."

Introduction

Why Mountains?

This book is titled 'Confronting Your Mountains' because trials, obstacles, and storms can sometimes look like mountains blocking the path of your purpose. Anu and I have always desired to write a book that will encourage not only our immediate family but everyone. This book talks about addictions, the strongholds that stagnate the journey of where God wants you to be. His desire is for you to be fruitful and successful. For those battling to prevail over addictions like pornography, alcohol, fear, pride, deceptions, or any other thing that has control over you. If you are struggling with addictions, be at peace, knowing that God's faithfulness is greater than your weakness. And, in that weakness, He will make you strong. Turn to Him today in prayer and ask Him for the strength to overcome! Every chapter in this book will reinforce the power of God and remind you that He is the only one capable of changing you. Let's pray.

Lord God, we put this prayer to you in the name of Jesus for those who have mountains, their addictions which they are finding hard to move. Eternal God, break their chains of addictions, blast away their mountains so they can see your glory. Let them feel your loving power and your kindness, goodness, and mercy. Thank you, loving God, for moving to answer this prayer request in no other name but Jesus' name. Amen.

We are moved to put this prayer request because we know what prayer can do. Moving on, this book contains prayer, Bible scriptures, and testimonies of God's transformation.

There are Bible solutions that will help you through the channels of God to make you a victor in your battles. Ultimately, this book aims to encourage, uplift, motivate and counsel, exposing you to the spiritual facts that God is not slack concerning the promises He has made to you and me. God really cares about you and wants to see your chains falling off. He wants to shut the mouths of the lions in your den, but you need to give Him access to do that by inviting Him into your life. What you need to do is put yourself in the master's hands for a transformation. When you finish reading this book, you will realize that God has great plans for you and doesn't want you to be oppressed or in bondag

Chapter One

There is Power in the Name of Jesus

There is power in the name of Jesus to break every chain, it doesn't matter how long you have been in the situation, and it doesn't make a difference how long you have been held down, God will break the chains off you. Certainly, God will.

There are lots of diverse things that people face today, ranging from battles with money, battles with drugs, weight issues, unforgiveness, and many more issues. These battles are not against flesh and blood but against principalities (Ephesians 6:12).

The battles that you are confronted with will only take the power of Jesus to fight them off; you don't have to fight on your own. The chains will fall if you let Jesus take up your battles.

1st Chronicle chapter 20: 17 says, "You will not have to fight this battle. Take up your positions; stand firm and see the deliverance the LORD will give you, Judah, and Jerusalem. Do not be afraid; do not be discouraged. Go out to face them tomorrow, and the LORD will be with you." The Lord God is saying you must take your position and stand still to see and witness how He will

1

deliver you from trouble. Sometimes in the thick of the storm, you might worry and wonder if God is still with you. Let me tell you a secret, He never left. The challenges you are going through have taken your focus off Him and on the size of the storm which is coming at you. If you must win this battle, never take your eyes off the Saviour. No matter how big the challenge, God is bigger. Those mountains can be surmounted. Those problems can be fixed, and your peace can be restored. But you must hand over the battle to the Lord.

He wants to deliver you, God is knocking on the door of your heart to let Him in, but you are holding on to anger and blaming those whom you feel have put you in the situation. But God is still knocking, will you let Him in? The question is, what is holding you from letting go and letting the power of Jesus scoop you from your pain? Stand up! and take your position as God intended you to do. First, you need to forgive yourself for what you put yourself through. Sometimes the pain is hard, and everywhere you turn, there are reminders all around you; it reminds you of the pain and how it diminished you.

Also, it's understandable that when you have been bruised and broken and scars are left behind, it can be difficult to comprehend. The songs say, *'who feels it knows it.'* Absolutely, that can be the case. But be reminded that there is power in the name of Jesus to break every chain. The only way that chain can fall off is through the powerful name of Jesus. No one can turn your sorrow into joy. Jesus; heals the broken-hearted and sets those that are in bondage free. All you have to do is exercise faith in Him. Remember, if you have faith like a mustard seed, you will be able to move mountains (Matthew 17:20). I know you may say it sounds easy, but it is hard. God says with Him all things are possible. Yes, this little faith, like a mustard seed mentioned in the book of Matthew, can do wonders. The word of God works, and it works for good for those who trust and have faith in Him. Romans 8:28 says, "And we know that all things work together for good to them that love God, to them who are the called according to his purpose." Letting go of everything, and letting God take charge shows that you trust Him."

The power to break every chain has been made available for you. All you need to do is to shout the name of Jesus to activate the power. No demon from Hell can stand when the name of Jesus is mentioned. At the mention of His name, things happen for the greater good. Meaning it alleviates darkness, and light takes dominance. With that, I would share with you how I asked God for His help to break free from my shackles.

First, I asked God for His forgiveness, and I asked Him to help me forgive those who have hurt me. The next thing I did was to set time for the Lord. There are days when I pray 10- 20 times a day with the Lord; these are times I allocated to pour my heart into the Lord God because I wanted to see the chains broken. Not that I am here to boast of myself or make you think I am perfect, but because I want you to know it's possible for those chains to fall. God wants you to be free, and today is the day to start the process of wanting to know God.

The time is ripe to go through the process where God can heal you and break down your mountains. Like Naaman, the leper. he had to go through the process in order to be healed by God. God wants to transform you like Abraham, Peter, Esther, Rahab, King David, and others. He wants to give you the spiritual mantle like Elisha. The world cannot give you the freedom and peace you crave because the world doesn't have it to give. Get to know God, and you will enjoy the benefits that come with His presence. When you know God for yourself, it will be easier for you to serve Him. God wants to know you on a personal level. He wants to set you free and help you live a wonderful life. Set the time to get acquainted with God today.

Chapter Two

Addictions

Call it by its name, addiction! A condition of being addicted to a certain activity. For some, it is a hard nut to crack. Your addiction may incapacitate you and make you vulnerable. The more you try to come out of it, the more it seems to be an obstacle preventing you from having that deliverance. It is like mountaineers trying to climb Kilimanjaro but cannot get that breakthrough because that mountain is difficult to climb, just like your addiction, so difficult to get rid of.

I want you to now grab your notebook and write down Philippians 4:13 "you can do all things not something but **all** things through Christ Jesus who strengthens you." There are times in your life when you feel as though you don't need to change. You've tried before, you've sought help, you've tried therapy, tried counselling, and even changed locations but you still find yourself back where you started.

Trying again no longer makes sense because of your past failures. I feel your pain and anxiety, but I am here to tell you there is hope. Try again with God. There is no failure when you try with God, He is the restorer of wasted years. It's tough to believe sometimes whether God is going to change you or not, but He will; that's why He wants you to come just as you are. It was challenging for me to believe. I spent my younger years pessimistic and believing that things would stay the same. It was inevitable; my life is just supposed to be that way – or so I thought.

A few weeks ago, I had a Sabbath school meeting; we were talking about King Ahaz; he decided that he was going to go against his father's wishes, he wasn't going to follow God, and he was going to practice his own ways. Due to the practice of his own ways, many of his sons died through sacrifice. From the lesson of King Ahaz, I learned from my own reasoning that when we practice our addiction, even though we do it in private or we feel like we are not affecting others, we are. King Ahaz killed his sons for a ritual; imagine how the wives might have felt. The mothers who spent years being in the king's company when they conceived knew that it was never certain for their sons because it was all about Ahaz's sacrifices to his gods. King Ahaz brought a lot of pain and agony to everyone around him.

I want you to think for a moment, who have you hurt whilst you've faced your addiction alone? When we decide to go the wrong path, others feel the pain as well. King Ahaz was a stubborn man whose addiction hurt others.

This coming month, I spent time writing my portion of this book; I started to think about my life; why do I tend to spend time away from God? What's stopping me? I created this analogy as I was questioning myself. King Ahaz knew about God, God was taught in his household by his father, but when trouble came, King Ahaz focused on rituals and magicians in his court rather than God.

I want to give you an example of a room; I picture you in that room, you know that you're room is dirty, there are clothes on the floor, clothes on the chair, and your bed is covered with clothes! It's horrible, and it's hard for you to walk through. Instead of cleaning the clothes, placing the dirty clothes in the wash and the clean clothes in your drawer, you decide to shift your clothes; when you need to go to your bed, you pick up the clothes and put them on the chair. When it's time to sit on the chair, you remove the clothes off the chair and put them on the bed. This goes on to become a pattern, but the solution is simple – go and wash the dirty clothes and go and fold and put away the clean clothes. I pondered on this analogy. How does this relate to you? Often-times, when you are so deep in your addiction, you make a routine. It's okay that we give in to our addictions every time we feel like it because we have not been taught in doing so, or we think, who cares, you need your fix, make babies with different fathers or mothers who are not always there, do all sorts of things because it is your life, but always remember you are hurting not just yourself but those in your circle; sometimes even those out of your circle. Think carefully.

Sometimes it feels like you have to keep picking up a pile of clothes and putting it somewhere else. This is you with your addiction running and ruining your life. You don't need to fail anymore; you can be victorious. You can change. God can change you. Yes, He can. God hears you; He says that it's your time. It's your time to receive your blessing, you deserve that extension in your life, and you deserve to have freedom from your addiction.

God will redesign your life, so much so that it will be an amazing transformation. Why? How? Because He loves you. How do I know? Well, once upon a time, I was sad, lonely, anxious, and vulnerable, and God has changed me, and He's given me so much. At the start of my late 30s, I had nothing, no confidence; I didn't believe in the future. I didn't want a future. I wanted to be that tree that doesn't bear anything but still wanted to get the best sunlight. In order words, I did not want to put any interest in God but still want God to bless me. God says draw near, and He will draw nearer. There is nothing difficult that God can't do. He is able; He mended me when I believed that I was too broken, too messed up, and too much of a failure for Him to help me.

This book will not only make you become aware of your addiction, but it will bring you back to focus. That's a promise. When we are addicted to something, we lose focus because the only thing we focus on is fulfilling our desire.

I want to share something I've realised. It was on a Saturday night, after Sabbath, I decided to indulge in something that I shouldn't. I believe that it was okay. I thought I was strong, and I convinced myself, just one more, but that one more added up, and soon enough, I was 40 pounds heavier, more depressed, and

8

angrier. Even though food obsession may not be the root of my addiction, that's how it started; we believe that we are strong enough for one more high, one more speed, one more sex with that person who doesn't care about you, and one more pornography video. But that one more can become dangerous to your soul. Let Jesus be the one more in your life, and He will turn things around for you.

Some of the addictions that can cause havoc in your lives

Sexual Addictions

Sexual addiction is like any other addiction out there. It is difficult when you are so encumbered with addiction and sometimes afraid to ask for help to avoid being judged. Just like King David struggled with lust in the Bible, there are real people in this world who are struggling with these types of addictions and feel ashamed to seek for help. But I am here to remind you that God can set you free, just call on Him, He is closer than you think.

Pornography addiction

For those who are trapped in pornography, it can be a difficult desire to let go of. But that stronghold can be broken. Pornography was known to the locals as a blue movie as I can remember as a child back then, it was relatively a new thing. Now, it is a big thing; the Bible does not specifically talk about pornography; however, the Bible talks about sexual immorality, and pornography fits right under the umbrella of it. Moreover, the Bible provides philosophical advice on the moral rot from the desire to pursue this kind of lifestyle. This kind of lifestyle is not profitable; it can never change you for the better; it only brings you down and sends all sorts of images into your head.

Some people think there is nothing wrong with looking at people having sex, for them, it is natural and cool. It gives a bit of spice to their relationship. But looking at such things can lead to other things. It can cause a man or woman to become unfaithful. It is just a distraction to the mind, and God doesn't like when we are lost in situations that distract our mind and prevent us from knowing Him.

There are many stories of individuals whose desire to look at pornographic movies has cost them their marriages and torn their families apart. There are those who see it as joy and fulfilment, but this sort of addiction doesn't bring joy but brokenness.

There are genuine people out there who are crying their hearts out to stop this addiction. For them, they are trapped; there is no way out. They have been watching pornography for so long that it has become part of them, yet they still want to stop. This message is for you, God can take away that unholy desire. He can help you. He heals those that are wounded and will set those trapped free, don't just sit there, and watch your life waste away. Pornography is not healthy for your mind. God will help you out; it may take a while but trust God, He will pull you through it all.

Your chains will fall down; they will be broken, and you will hear the chains falling. Look at the example of King David as mentioned: at some point in his life, he lusted after the flesh, and he turned this lust into a reality by going after the wife of Uriah. Uriah was a faithful man in King David's Army, very honourable and respectable. He had a beautiful wife named Bathsheba; this woman was beautiful, and extremely appealing. One day, she was out in her courtyard, maybe not to expose herself, she was just about to have a shower; well, the eyes of King David caught her; I will leapfrog here, and guess what, King David lusted after Bathsheba and pursued her. But in the end, King David's lack of control (lust) caused pain to everyone involved. (the story is in the books of 2nd Samuel and 1st Kings).

But when David confessed his sin to God, there was forgiveness from the Lord. Like David, bring your sin to God, you don't have to hide it from Him, He already knows. Proverbs 28:13 says, "Whoever conceals his transgressions will not prosper, but he who confesses and forsakes them will obtain mercy."

Chapter Three

God can free you from sexual desires.

One thing we need to know is that the Bible offers hope to those who struggle with strongholds. The Bible is all about breaking the chains. God's word is super powerful. First Corinthians 10:13 says, "No temptation has overtaken you except what is common to mankind. And God is faithful; he will not let you be tempted beyond what you can bear. But when you are tempted, he will also provide a way out so that you can endure it."

1st John 1:9, says "If we confess our sins, he is faithful and just and will forgive us our sins and purify us from all righteousness." 1 John 2:15-17 says, "Do not love the world or the things in the world. If anyone loves the world, the love of the Father is not in him. For all that is in the world—the desires of the flesh and the desires of the eyes and pride in possessions—is not from the Father but is from the world. And the world is passing away along with its desires, but whoever does the will of God abides forever." Matthew 5:6 affirms the verses in 1, John, by saying, "Blessed are those who hunger and thirst for righteousness, for they shall be satisfied." God's words here demonstrate that He is able to free us from all addictions and strongholds; anything that pesters our minds and hinders our relationship with Him. At this present moment, why not take the initial step and write down all your pain and desire of wanting to change?

_____

_____

_____

_____

_____

_____

_____

_____

_____

_____

_____

_____

_____

_____

_____

_____

_____

_____

_____

_____

Additionally, I want you to have physical evidence of what you were before God transformed you. The sexual addiction you are facing now may be difficult, and it may be completely unbearable, but once you walk through with God, it's worth it.

When I was facing my addiction, I couldn't believe it. Sometimes I felt selfish because I slipped up even though I prayed to God an hour ago, pleading for His help to stop. My addiction here was playing the lottery gambling because I love maths, so I would say to myself, I am playing with numbers. I would diligently look at the lottery numbers and explore them like a book. I used to be in my own element, and I thought it felt good. I would sit from Saturday early in the morning to sundown, and I was convinced I was doing the right thing. I was winning, but I was losing God; I had no time for Him. My prayer was a drive-by prayer.

Oh, how foolish I was, having little time for God and wasting my money thinking that I was going to win the lottery one day. If I did not have the money to play the lottery, I would be satisfied but the next time when the money is around I would really go beyond my budget hoping to win.

Addiction can be so ferocious in one's life; you can do anything out of the ordinary to maintain that fix. I felt as though I couldn't break free.

Hope didn't exist but now even if I relapse, I remember a special text (scripture) in Psalms 138: 6-8 "Though the Lord be high, yet hath respect unto the lowly: but the proud he knoweth afar off. Though I walk in the midst of trouble, thou wilt revives me: thou shalt stretch forth thine hand against the wrath of mine enemies, and thy right hand shall save me.

"The Lord will perfect that which concerneth me: thy mercy, O Lord, endureth forever: forsake not the works of thine own hands." There is always hope in Christ. If we allow ourselves hope, our outcomes become better. Thank God for those who were praying for me.

God's hope isn't like our hope. Hope is not like a film, after you watch the film and it finally disappears from your brain, you don't feel as happy as you felt once you watched it in the theatre or in your home. God's hope is a promise, a promise that will never fail. A promise that is not bound by how good or holy you are.

Jeremiah 29:11 (GNB) says, "I alone know the plans I have for you, plans to bring you prosperity and not disaster, plans to bring about the future you hope for." I want you to allow the Lord to provide the plan, He has made specifically for you and His plan for you isn't to harm you or make you feel guilty about your addiction or your relapse. No! God's plan for you is to help you. His plan is bigger than what you know. It's bigger than you.

It's very hard to acknowledge this but whenever you feel low, just place God in the centre of your situation, hand over your life and worries to Him, and be assured that He is right there with you. Take a chance with God.

Chapter Four

It's time to stop

James 1: 14-15 (NIV) says, "but each person is tempted when they are dragged away by their own evil desire and enticed. Then, after their desire has been conceived, it gives birth to sin; and sin, when it is full-grown, gives birth to death." With your addition, you have to acknowledge that every one of us has the problem of temptation, some of the temptations might not hurt you in the beginning but over time, they will destroy you. James 1: 14-15 is telling you that if you ask God to stop the temptation before it happens, you wouldn't sin. It's very simple. We sin when we act on our temptation, to stop that temptation, God needs to intervene. Prayer is one way in which we can ask God to take away our temptation and that is exactly what I did. I began to pray earnestly to God, and whenever I was gripped by the desire to gamble, I kept the money for tithe and offering. One day I decided to prove to the Lord, by giving Him my entire wage (£350 pounds), and guess what God did? I received £800 from the company as a gesture of goodwill! God can be tested and trusted, He never fails.

The Lord God is able and willing to set you free, no matter the addiction. Be encouraged to pray.

Prayer

Dear God, you are God and God alone. The healer and restorer, a possibility, and a promise keeper. You are a strong tower, the righteous runs to you for safety. Oh, how excellent is your name above all the earth? At this present moment, I am asking you to help that person who is held down by an addiction they just cannot correct on their own. They are so lost and wounded, and spiritually crushed. God, I ask you in your mercy to follow them and delete the mess in their life. Reload them with the assurances of Jeremiah 29:11. Keep your will towards them may they always remember that your will towards them is of good and not of evil. Lord, please, touch them and deliver them in Jesus's name, Amen.

Be patient with what you are going through.
Romans 12:12 (ESV) says "Rejoice in hope, be patient in tribulation, be constant in prayer." Right now, I want us to be *constant in prayer* because prayer is power. It's our time to speak to God, one to one. It's a time when we should allow the spirit to come down so we can speak to *Him*.

Just like Jesus when He said, " We too need to speak to our father." Even though right now we are praying because we are in pain, or we know that it's time to surrender our addiction to Christ. I want you to reflect, write down your lowest point and ask God how you would like him to intervene: begin to write your own prayer to God.

Dear God in the name of Jesus:

_____

_____

_____

_____

_____

_____

_____

_____

_____

_____

_____

_____

_____

_____

_____

_____

_____

_____

_____

_____

_____

Chapter Five

Money: Has it become a Strong Hold?

Jesus stated in the parable "it will be easier for a camel to pass through the eye of a needle than rich man to enter heaven."

Money

We will hear what the Bible says about money.

1 Timothy 6:6-12 says "But godliness with contentment is great gain, or we brought nothing into the world, and we cannot take anything out of the world. But if we have food and clothing, with these we will be content. But those who desire to be rich fall into temptation, into a snare, into many senseless and harmful desires that plunge people into ruin and destruction. For the love of money is the root of all kinds of evil. It is through this craving that some have wandered away from the faith and pierced themselves with many pangs."

But as for you, O man of God, flee these things. Pursue right-eousness, godliness, faith, love, steadfastness, and gentleness. Fight the good fight of the faith. Take hold of the eternal life to which you were called and about which you made the good confession in the presence of many witnesses." And in Ecclesiastes 5:10 "He who loves money will not be satisfied with money, nor he who loves wealth with his income; this also is vanity." "No one can serve two masters, for either he will hate the one and love the other, or he will be devoted to the one and despise the other."

Matthew 22:7 "You cannot serve God and money. You will either love one or hate the other

Hebrews 13:5 "Keep your life free from love of money, and be content with what you have, for he has said, "I will never leave you nor forsake you."

Please, do not be confused, God is not against us being wealthy or rich. In fact, the book of Proverbs 10:22 says, "The blessing of the Lord makes rich, and He adds no sorrow with it." God is only advising us not to make money an idol. We shouldn't let money separate us from the love of God, the pursuit of money shouldn't take us away from the presence of God. When the desire to be wealthy controls your thought and actions, it then becomes a stronghold. God desires that we prosper (be wealthy) and be in good health, but He wants us to do it in accordance with His purpose and guidance. The Lord God said, "you shall remember Him, for it is he who gives you the power to get wealth, that He may confirm His covenant that He swore to your fathers, as it is this day (Deuteronomy 8:18)." From the above scriptures, we can see that God is the One who blesses us with wealth, next time you look at your money, remember God is the One who provided it. So, don't hesitate to give Him thanks and worship Him in spirit and in truth.

Money is good. Everything that comes from the Lord is good, but if we are not careful, our heart posture towards money can become evil. When the Bible says the love of money is the root of all evil, it was referring to the obsession with material gain. When a person is obsessed with acquiring wealth, they will want more and more money, their interest will be solely on money and as a result, something else will suffer whether it be their relationship with their family, God, and even themselves. Money will become their god. because anything you put before the Creator will become your god.

There are so many cases where the love of money has cost people their lives. Look at the story of Ananias and Safari, in Acts 5:1-11 "But a certain man named Ananias, with Sapphira his wife, sold a possession and kept back part of the price, his wife also being privy to it, and brought a certain part, and laid it at the apostles' feet. But Peter said, Ananias, why hath Satan filled thine heart to lie to the Holy Ghost and to keep back part of the price of the land? Whiles it remained, was it not thine own? And after it was sold, was it not in thine own power? Why hast thou conceived this thing in thine heart? Thou hast not lied unto men, but unto God. And Ananias hearing these words fell down and gave up the ghost: and great fear came on all of them that heard these things. And the young men arose, wound him up, carried him out, and buried him. And it was about the space of three hours after, when his wife, not knowing what was done, came in. And Peter answered unto her, tell me whether ye sold the land for so much? And she said, Yea, for so much. Then Peter said unto her, how is it that ye have agreed together to tempt the Spirit of the Lord? behold, the feet of them which have buried thy husband are at the door and shall carry thee out. Then fell she down straightway at his feet and yielded up the ghost: and the young men came in, and found her dead, and, carrying her forth, buried her by her husband. And great fear came upon all the church, and upon as many as heard these things." The love of money cost two people their lives. When money becomes a stronghold, things can go terribly wrong.

There is nothing wrong with having money, and it is advisable to work towards being financially stable. But if by any chance, money becomes a stumbling block in your relationship with God, then you need an urgent spiritual operation. You need God's divine intervention to break the stronghold of money over your life because it will profit you nothing if you gain the whole world and lose your soul. Let's pause and have a look at Proverbs 21:5: "The plans of the diligent lead surely to abundance, but everyone who is hasty comes only to poverty."

"Do not be anxious about anything, but in everything by prayer and supplication with thanksgiving let your requests be made known to God (Philippians 4:6)." Beloved, God has good intentions for you. When you are beset by financial troubles, don't get into panic mode. Rest in the promises of God, and trust Him to give you the wisdom to fix it. Remember, "A faithful man will abound with blessings, but whoever hastens to be rich will not go unpunished (Proverbs 28:20)." Don't compromise your values or principles to make ends meet, that is what the devil desires, don't let him win.

Sometimes you tell yourself I will come out of it, but it is only for a short time then it becomes longer than you imagine. In the process, you lose your integrity, values, and beliefs. This is what the enemy, the devil, desires for you to destroy your purpose and the greatness of what God has for you. There are times when you do realize what you are doing has no benefit just pure pain and stress, but your addiction is overpowering, And life becomes worse than when you first started. The good news is the chain breaker is here to rescue you and can give you a clean slate. But you must be willing to give Him your all. The chains of money are not always easy to break because the world has glorified money. As my friend would say money is an attraction for many.

At the age of ten months, my baby could tell the difference between money and paper. First, I gave her a piece of paper and she tore it. Next, I gave her a ten-pound note but she did not tear it. You might think if I had tried it a second time maybe she would have torn it, who knows? But she did not. This just shows us the importance attached to money. I want you to pause here and make God the first in everything.

Moving on, let me reiterate that God can help you. If you give God the okay to help, He will bring peace to your soul. Some people might try to convince you otherwise but be guaranteed that

God has the number one place in your life, and not the love for money.

Prove God

"Honour the Lord with your wealth and with the first fruits of all your produce; then your barns will be filled with plenty, and your vats will be bursting with wine (Proverbs 3:9 -10)."

I want you to prove to God that when you receive any earnings give it to God first as a tithe offering. If you don't go to church find someone that is less financially stable and give as the Spirit of God leads you. And then you will see the blessings of the Lord manifest.

Chapter Six

Testimony

I remember having no money during covid-19 and that was the period the battle began. Back then when I was broke, I would play the lottery and I always win money. But deep down I didn't want to live like that. I didn't want to depend on gambling for survival. I wanted to set good examples for my children and those around me. I could hear two voices nudging me in different directions; one telling me to remain in my old ways, and the other asking me to trust God for a job. The second voice reminded me that the cattle on the hills and grains on the field belong to God.

The longer I listened to that voice, the more I believed it was the Holy Spirit. I was not going to fail that test because I know God has good intentions for me, and I wanted to see the manifestation of His power in my life. I remember a time when I had some lottery numbers and I called one of my good friends to ask her advice to play the lottery that day, but I couldn't reach her and concluded she must have been busy. So, I decided to listen to that quiet voice, and I didn't play the lottery. When the numbers later came up, I was like: "Jeez, I just missed out on millions." I honestly thought I had missed a blessing, but then the Holy Spirit reminded me that all power and wealth belong to God. And that very moment, I knew the stronghold of gambling out of my life was broken until this day. My heart is filled with peace.

You might be thinking that was a foolish decision but remember God is the restorer and giver of all things. I thought of those men and even women God took care of; like Elijah, Moses, Joshua, Abraham, and Esther, these individuals were tested but God helped them to pass their tests. God proved Himself to be a sure helper and deliverer, a rock of refuge that can be counted on at any time. He didn't fail those who trusted in Him in times past and would not fail me either. And truly God showed up for me, He blessed me with a job.

If you ever find yourself in a situation you cannot control, if you ever find yourself in financial difficulty, I want you to trust God. Believe in His words when He says He will help you, don't be afraid to cry out to Him or follow His instructions, I guarantee you, He will always show up for you. You might read this, and murmur *easier said than* done to yourself. But I want to remind you that with God, all things are possible.

Job was a man who lost everything. The only thing he had left was the boils on his body. It got to a point even his wife turned against him, and asked him to curse God and die. This is the devil's quick repair clothed in deception. He knows that if you cry out to God, He will hear you and help you. Thank God Job set a good example for us, he didn't give up, nor turn against God or allow the devil to win. He stood firm in his trust in God, he fought the good fight of faith. And God rewarded him beyond his wildest imagination; he got seven times over what he lost. Job was blessed with much more than what he first had.

Before Job's trial, the devil boasted that Job was only upright because God has blessed him, but even in the midst of his trial and suffering, Job still held on to God, putting the devil to shame. Standing up for the love of God gave Job victory. When those in trouble trust in God they shall never fail. Don't let the stress of the world define who you are. Money with wrong connotations has taken the lives of many because of hatred and greed. Evil has dominated the true essence of money. The lack of money has caused many to make decisions that affect the way people view them, and the way they live. Be wise, stand firm for God and He will bless, save and prosper you beyond your imagination. Why not take a chance with God and see how He works? I took a chance with God and all that I am seeing are the wonders of His blessings. I could go on and on about the stronghold money can have on our life; without God, it will have a negative impact but with God, it will be positive. Trust and obey God.

Chapter Seven

Trust and Obey

Trust

Trust in Him, trust in God, and He will guide you to all truth. When you are sad and lonely, still trust in God. When life challenges hit you from the left and right, tell those challenges your God is bigger, stronger, and mightier. Tell that problem, you are not a victim but a victor. Tell that stronghold you have been made more than a conqueror.

Life's challenges can seem overwhelming, but you've got a God who calms storms. He is a God of love and compassion, surrender your burdens to Him and watch Him speedily come through for you. Trust God, He is never late, He is always on time. His promises are true and sure – don't stop believing them.

Obedience

We must be obedient. When I was little, I was very stubborn. Obedience to me, at the time, was a system of control by my parents. I didn't want to be controlled, I wanted to do as I liked and wished. I used to think: *why do I need to obey my father and mother?*

What is the point of resting on the Sabbath? I had a lot of questions and I decided that I didn't want to obey because to obey meant someone wanted to control me. As I grew older, I realized obedience wasn't a form of control but **protection.** I finally understood why my parents told me obedience was a good thing. They wanted to protect me from the consequences of bad decisions. Why would I want to go to places that will likely get me in trouble? Why would I want to do things that will ruin my character, reputation, and future? How was that going to make me better? It wasn't. I started to change my definition of obedience, I changed it from control to protection. God wants to protect you too. Putting God before your addiction is not control but protection. It may feel like control because it's hard for your body to stop thinking about your addiction, but God is in control.

Battling with your temptation is a difficult fight, but God is ready to fight with you and for you. Deuteronomy 13: 4 says, "It is the Lord your God you must follow, and Him you must revere. Keep his commands and obey Him; serve Him and hold fast to Him. It's part of our duty, to be obedient. I have recognized my duty from the years of trusting and following God, and our only duty to God is to obey Him. By obeying Him, we are serving Him. Deuteronomy 13:4 states "and hold fast to Him", this week, you are going to stop your addiction, your addiction will have no control over you in these incoming days. But remember to hold fast to God. His promise to help you when the temptation to disobey arises. Remember that by His help you can do anything (Philippians 4:13).

"Disobedience often hurts others," a phrase I've heard my whole life but now I really understand what it means. When you're addicted, you automatically put yourself first, you don't think of others. Sometimes you try to tell yourself that your addiction isn't hurting anyone but when you have a proper conversation with your family and friends, you realise you are hurting them. An example of how we hurt others when we choose not to follow God. An example is found in Jonah 1:4-11, verse 10. Jonah escaped his duties; he did not want to travel to Nineveh. He was disobedient and he travelled on the boat to escape from his duties. Jonah 1:4-11, verse 10 says, "This terrified them and they asked, 'What have you done?"

In this verse, Jonah risked the lives of the men on the boat. God had spared them in the end but if it weren't for God's mercy Jonah the lives of the men on the boat with Jonah would be in total lost. If we repent, just like Jonah and we say to ourselves that we will do as God pleases, we wouldn't hurt others.

Feeding your addictions (sin) in the dark, or in the open is dreadful because there are others who get hurt in the process. You might think your addiction is a form of escape from the hard blows of life, you might feel asking for help is giving others access to control you, you may be struggling with the guilt of addiction; thinking you've let yourself and others down, but help is here. Jesus is willing to help you, like Peter when he was sinking, Jesus stretched His hand. He is stretching His hand to you today. You might have become comfortable in your comfort zone and accepted the description of yourself. Yes, you may be perceived that way but with God it is different. God is saying, "Child I look at you differently. Not as the world looks at you. I look at you as my child, and I am willing and ready to fix you permanently."

Please, stretch your hand to God and let Him pull you out of whatever mess you've made. Jonah 3:7-10 shows us that when we repent and turn to God in obedience, He will help us and bless us. In Jonah 3:7 -8, the king makes a decree that no animal or human should eat, or drink unless they give up their evil ways. In the end, they repented of their evil ways and God was merciful to them (Jonah 3:10). Just like Jonah, before he too repented, there will be those who think you don't deserve mercy, or you are not worth the change. But I want to tell you God is the one who calls the shots, He's in charge and doesn't need the opinion of others to help you. It doesn't matter what people think, say, or do, God decides.

You will begin to reap the benefits of obedience once you start practicing it. Jesus says in Luke 11:28 (GWT), "Jesus replied, ' Rather, how blessed are those who hear and obey God's word.'" When we become obedient, we attract blessings to our lives.

In your darkness, God will come through

Don't allow the darkness that comes with your addiction to cloud your decision to read this book. Instead, ask God to help you push through this book. Ask Him to guide you through the pages, ask for change, and to change your life for the better. Remember, it's not dark when God is with us.

Chapter Eight

The landing

Can I really change?

You may have been battling with addiction for years, you may think you are long gone from your addiction. Perhaps you are known as a smoker or womanizer, and you are thinking since everyone knows who you are, why should you bother? Why should you change? Why should you even try? You should change because you are more than this. God didn't create you to waste your life on top of women or men you can barely remember their names when the night is over. God didn't create you to waste away in the haze of euphoria that only has the illusion to offer. You were made for much more.

You were created to live for a purpose and make an impact, generations are waiting to see your light. Don't trade it for a fickle title. You've got a glorious destiny, don't waste it on cracks and alcohol. The only way to change is by allowing God to help you make that change. In my journey, the Holy Spirit has been a solid helper. I asked Him to remove anything that is not of God from me, and He did. As I read and meditated on Scripture every day, I began to see the changes. The more I communicated with God (prayed), the more I began to walk in His purpose. And to His glory, I am no longer where I was, I can see God's intervention in my life. His awesome plans for me have begun to manifest and more than ever, I am convinced that His eyes are on me, guiding and leading me, I don't walk amiss.

Prayer is a powerful tool; the more I prayed, the more I could see the love of God flowing within me. I began to pray to God and asked for His divine help. Psalms 51 and 119 were the Psalms I incorporated into my journey with God. Today, I want to prepare you for the landing. The landing that God has promised for all of us when we are with Him.

Growing up, I have always loved God and desired to serve Him. I knew about Him, but I wasn't fully ready to commit to Him. At that time, I wanted to do my own thing, and have my own way. You too may want to serve God, but guilt, shame, and addictions are holding you back. I come to tell you that God can break those strongholds – no matter what it is. God is willing to help you, hang in there. He will definitely help you.

In the last quarter of 2014, I decided to dedicate my time to reading the Bible from start to finish. In August, I finished the book of Genesis and was excited to read about Moses. He was my favourite prophet as a child, and so I was excited to know who he truly was. I had watched many adaptations of the story of Moses before then, but the Biblical account held my attention. Did you know that Moses wasn't ready to change? No, I didn't either. I was shocked. Moses's shy nature reminded me of who I am. There were times when people wanted me to do things either for my benefit or theirs, but I was too scared to budge. Right now, you might feel unprepared to fight your addiction, but God has chosen you, and He is gracing you with strength and courage. He's tired of watching you fly around aimlessly and wants to guide your landing.

Moses questioning God is a reflection of who I was, and who you are now. Because you still feel the pain in your body, you think you will never be healed. But let me remind you that Moses never saw himself as a speaker, he was scared and didn't have the boldness to take God's message to Pharaoh, and the spirit of "what if" had him suggesting alternatives.

I am trying to tell you that change isn't glamorous, you don't start perfect and get perfect, no. Sometimes we start bad, with baggage, sadness in our hearts, and fear, but God says, "come to me anyone who is heavily laden, and I will give you rest."

Moses in the end was able to part the sea and protect his people by praying to God. Yes, there were obstacles in his way and unfortunate things happened, but God was there. That's the difference. Moses was no longer scared because he saw the change, God changed him from an unsure stutterer into a confident leader. Moses was so close to God, his face literally glowed after conversing with Him. Can you imagine the relationship they had? Moses was talking to the most powerful one, the *Creator*!

If God can talk to a young man who was the son of a servant, a child who lived in the palace knowing he was different, and then ended up in self-exile then why can't we have that? Some of us might have similar backgrounds to Moses. You might have been raised by people who were not your parents, you might have struggled to fit in, knowing that you will never belong. You might have been seen as the outcast, the no-good, but God wants you to know that He cares. He sees you, loves you, and wants a relationship with you. He wants to help you change.

Moses' origins (Numbers 26:58-61).

"These are the families of the Levites: the family of the Libnites, the family of the Hebronites, the family of the Mahlites, the family of the Mushites, the family of the Korathites. And Kohath begat Amram. And the name of Amram's wife was Jochebed, the daughter of Levi, whom her mother bare to Levi in Egypt: and she bares unto Amram, Aaron and Moses, and Miriam their sister.

And unto Aaron was born Nadab, and Abihu, Eleazar, and Ithamar. And Nadab and Abihu died when they offered strange fire before the LORD."

It's time to change.

Sometimes when we sin or cut short the glory of God, we become guilt-ridden and shame-faced and feel unworthy of God's presence. We become shameful of our 'uncleanness' and like Jonah, we decide to run away from God's presence, but away from the presence of God is where the danger lies. When your clothes get stained, you don't hide them in the dustbin, you take them to the laundry. When we sin, we shouldn't run from God. Rather go to Him, confess all and ask for His strength. His strength will help us not to fall into sin again.

Your addiction might have become a storm you can no longer control, but the One who calms the storms is knocking on your door, let Him in. "Behold, I stand at the door and knock: if any man hears my voice, and opens the door, I will come into him and will sup with him, and he with me (Revelation 3:20)." Why do you fight on your own, you will not win. Ephesians says, "for we wrestle not against flesh and blood, but against principalities, against powers, against the rulers of the darkness of this world, against spiritual wickedness in high places." The battle is not yours it is the Lord's He is the winner. So, give yourselves completely to God. Come near to God, and God will come nearer to you. God is mighty in battle stay focus and lean on God. God's plans for you are good and not evil. That is the honest truth. Your journey might be rocky and so many hurdles in your way you cannot think properly take a moment and seek God, and try Him. I have tried God many times and He has always come through for me.

Chapter Nine

God forgives and He will forgive you.

I want you to know that God forgives. You might feel you've gotten too deep into sin and unworthy of forgiveness, but I am here to tell you God is willing to forgive you. No matter how deep you are in the mess, God is ready to pull you out and wash you clean. He is a loving, kind, and patient God who doesn't hold our faults against us. He will bind up your wounds, and break the stronghold of your addiction (Isaiah 49:24).

In the first part of Psalms 103: 3, the Bible says, "He who forgives all your iniquities." it might be hard to believe that, but God *will* forgive *you*. If you confess to Him (1 John 1:9). He won't just forgive you of some sins but **all!** Jesus Christ even while He hung from the cross, said to the Father, "Father, forgive them for they know not what they do." What greater proof is there to show that God cares for you and me? Surrender to Him today, and He will heal your broken heart.

What does God want from us?

Colossians 3:12-13 says: "Therefore, as the elect of God, holy and beloved, put on tender mercies, kindness, humility, meekness, longsuffering; bearing with one another, and forgiving one another, if anyone has a complaint against another; even as Christ forgave you, so you also must do."

Prayer is a one-on-one conversation with God.

Romans 12: 12 (GNB) says, "Let your hope keep you joyful, be patient in your troubles, and pray at all times." In times of crisis, prayer is what you need. Pray during your good times and your bad times, pray without ceasing. The bewilderment you are experiencing, causing you to think there is no way out, can be solved with prayers. Prayer is a weapon that helps you dismantle the plans of the devil, and gives you the freedom to find peace and rest in the Lord. Romans 12: 12 says "pray at all times" when we pray at all times, we will see changes in our lives. Prayer is the most intimate form of affection we can give to the Lord. We can go to the Lord, and cry to Him when there's no one to lean on, we can pour our heart to Him. Prayer gives God "permission" to intervene in our lives. The first step in prayer is talking and the second step is believing. When you pray, you must place your entire hope on Christ. Even when you can't see the light, you must keep walking with Christ until you get to the end.

A huge part of the landing is recognising the power of *prayer,* and how it fuels your relationship with God.

Whenever the weight of life threatens to overwhelm me, prayer keeps me rooted and anchored to God. There were times when I struggled, every waking day, I became anxious, impatient, angry, and bitter, all because I chose not to talk to God. But now I finally understand that He is ever ready to break down chains for me, you, and everyone else. I realized that by going down on my knees and asking God to help me stop worrying about my mountain. God is bigger than our mountains anyway, all He wants is for you to come home – to Him. God is waiting for you and desires to build a relationship with you, with the intention of giving you a better life. As Ezekiel 36:26 says "And I will give you a new heart, and a new spirit I will put within you. And I will remove the heart of stone from your flesh and give you a heart of flesh."

Ephesians 4:22-24 (ESV) says, "Put off your old self, which belongs to your former manner of life and is corrupt through deceitful desires, and to be renewed in the spirit of your minds, and to put on the new self, created after the likeness of God in true righteousness and holiness." Prayer is one of the first steps in changing your life for the better. Hebrews 4: 12 says, "For the word of God is alive and active. Sharper than any double-edged sword, it penetrates even to dividing soul and spirit, joints, and marrow; it judges the thoughts and attitudes of the heart." I want you to take this time, to seek reverence with God, and talk to Him about your problems, your pain, your mountain, and how your bad habits are harming you to the point where you can no longer recognise yourself. I have created a sample prayer if you don't know how to pray, or do not know what to pray for. Say the Lord's prayer in Matthew 6:9-13, "Our Father in heaven, hallowed be your name, your kingdom come, you will be done, on earth as it is in heaven. Give us today our daily bread. And forgive us our debts, as we also have forgiven our debtors. And lead us not into temptation but deliver us from the evil one."

Chapter Ten

Giving up is not allowed

God has called you and He says giving up is not welcomed. Never. Why? Because He has a purpose for your life, a glorious one. Do not try to give up or end your life because of the poor decisions you've made. It doesn't matter if you made them whilst knowing Christ or when you didn't, God is not interested in the state of your laundry, no. He wants you to come to the understanding that all things are possible with Him. No matter what anyone may think or say to you. If your desire is to take a stand for God, I encourage you to blow your trumpet and sing hosanna. Let no one stop you from becoming who God has designed you to be, "for His plans towards you is for your welfare, and not for evil, to give you a future and a hope (Jeremiah 29: 11, ESV)."

Taste and see that the Lord is good, His mercy endures forever. That was David's experience with God. The story of David as some of us know, he became King by the anointing of God. David was the last son of Jesse when the prophet Samuel anointed him. David walks with God through God's anointing. David was able to have that faith in God to defeat the philistines and bring hope to the Israelites. When David defeated the philistines that did not go so well with King Saul because at that time, he was the Israelite King. The people were so happy that David defeated the philistines, they dance, and shout *"David killed ten thousand while King Saul killed one thousand"*. That grieved King Saul's heart therefore jealousy began to creep into his heart toward David. (the story is in 1 Samuel 17:57 and 18:16) But God deliver David from Saul, and David became the King of Israel. Wow! God is wonderful He can deliver you from your addiction.

Seek refuge in Christ

The keyword "**refuge**" is identified as a form of staying safe and taking shelter from God to keep you safe from danger; it is anything that has the potential to harm you. seeking refuge in Christ Jesus and staying in His company. He is our protection from danger and trouble. He delivers us with shelter in the midst of adversity. Psalms 46: 1 (GNB) says "God is our shelter and strength, always ready to help in times of trouble." Wherever you are right now, whether you feel hopeless, you're in trouble, there is nothing in this world that can impress you, you've practiced meditation, exercise, or sports to get your troubles out of your head, you've eaten through your entire foods in your fridge because you're just so tired of your life. You feel like you want to do things on your own. But things are turning not so good for you, you started to practice things in order to serve your own pleasure.

Your own pleasure can be anything that is not in accordance with God's principles like drugs alcohol sexual desires. For me, my own pleasure as mentioned would be playing the lottery. Watching shows on the sabbath because I wanted to, this was the first sign, at that time, go to parties and dance my heart out. I remember coming out of the show with my husband I dance so much that I did not care about my spiritual walk. The morning living the show my husband and I were driving I think both of us fell asleep, I heard the Holy Spirit in my sleep say you are going to die to wake up when I open my eyes the vehicle was an inch away from colliding with a big wall in the road. God saved me that night. I was so happy he did. Another that Go

In life, there are so many things that trigger someone to go down a bad path, it could be bullying or any other impediment.

My story starts when I was a teen, I had problems with bullies. Anyone who wants to tear down your life, they are considered a bully. I spent years taking in their bullying, it was hard to process things, and I started not liking my life. All I wanted was love and acceptance. That was my void and, in most cases, people who are addicted are those who have never experienced *love*.

When love is not in the picture for some they can hold on to other things that they feel can fulfil their void. Food for me was a fix I used food to fix it and for many years I did. It came to a point that in my early 20s I was weighing, nearly 18 stone. I am 5'2, so imagine all of that weight on a small body. I thought that I loved myself, and I pretended to. But really, what had happened was that I was lying to myself. I didn't really like the way I look. I hated that I couldn't lose the weight. I saw my friends lose weight easily but for me, it was a struggle. Serving God was a challenge, I felt that I was not seeing His help I was so engulfed in the web of being overweight. I hated that feeling.

I used the words, hate a lot but I want to change that for you now. You might hate yourself or you might hate what others did to you. Amos 5:15 (GNB) says "Hate what is evil, love what is right, and see that justice prevails in the courts. Perhaps the LORD will be merciful to the people of this nation who are still left alive." For me, Amos taught me that I should 'hate what is evil', that didn't include me. I stopped using hate just because the scripture stated that. I started to think progressively. I was no longer going to say the word hate.

I decided that I was going to hate what was bad. As the years go by, I make a decision to stop thinking of not liking myself and choosing to exercise. I wanted my life to be constructive. How was I going to be constructive? ' I decided to seek refuge in God, I accepted that He is my shelter and strength (Psalms 46:1). I made a list, I stopped eating badly, even though physically I didn't want to read my Bible and pray, I started my prayer with some small steps. I realised at that time that I was scared. I feared changing myself. God eliminating my problems one step at a time, I was able to come out changed and produce this book for you. I prayed to God in my time of need, and I said, 'I don't know God what to do but please help me. I gave God the opportunity to work on me His hands became my shelter. His hands are sturdy, and His words He whispered into my ears are an encouragement. My mountains can never be bigger than me as long as I allow God to be my refuge and strength. For you who are going through these rough patches. Sometimes, you may be trying to have a relationship with God, but there are obstacles that will stand in the way making it hard to focus on God. Trust God He will help you stop thinking of how you going to get by with your struggles. You think the solution is to give up. But it does not need to be that way, God decides your path, a path that is much different from your outcome.

You may have picked up this book to find answers. The words of God in this book will lead you to the path where God wants you to be. God wants to shape and refine you. He wants to build you and change your life for the better. He has figured you out and all He wants is to redirect your pathway. "God is your shelter and strength (Psalms 46:1)." Yes, let Him be your shelter He will crumble your mountains. Your mountains won't stand a chance once the Lord is fighting for you. Stand! Still! And see! God Salvation!

Chapter Eleven

God sees you, He sees that you are in pain

God has seen you battle with your addiction in the dark. He sees you (Jeremiah 16:17 ESV). God sees all your struggles even when you hide under the covers. God sees it all (Hebrews 4: 13 ESV). There is nothing in this world that God doesn't see and right now God see's that you're in pain, your soul has been crying for Him for a long time. God is there to rescue you.

God wants to tell you that He is willing to fight for you, He wants you to come to Him and confess your sins. It says in 1st John 1:9 "But if we confess our sins to God, He is able and just to forgive us and purify us from all our wrongdoings." I want to tell you that your addictions do not define you when you choose to confess your sins to God.

You don't need to harm yourself or give up on your life because you can't control your addiction. God knows that you can't fight your own battles. God made it easy for everyone to come to Him in prayer. He hears your distress when you cry. Psalms 18:6 says, "In my distress, I called upon the Lord; I cried for help. From His temple, He heard my voice, and my cry to Him reached His ears."

Isaiah 41: 10 says "Fear not, for I am with you; be not dismayed, for I am your God; I will strengthen you, I will help you, I will uphold you with my righteous right hand." God is standing beside you, you just got to call Him. His light will cast down over you and you will see His magnificent light. Don't doubt Him. God always makes promises, and He keeps them. God reminds us, in His words that nothing is impossible with Him all things are super possible. God will run the extra mile for you. He will pick you up and bring you to the destination or goal He wants for your life, God will hold you up for as long as you want Him to. God never gives up on you, so don't give up on yourself, and if you feel as though there is no hope, and your words aren't working. I want to prove to you by just expressing your pain and explaining to God why you want to give up, ask God for three things you want from Him before you give up. Ask God to answer you, and say to God, "allow your will to be done in your life.

Small talk with God

Lord, I want to give up, I want to give up on myself, I want to give into my addiction, but I want you to show me how to change" and have faith in you!

God's power is above and greater than ours, it's more immense and powerful than we have ever experienced.

My short experience

I want to give you an anecdote about my life, there was a point in my life when I felt like life was not worth living, there was nothing right in my life. My grades were going down, my life felt messy and awkward, and I wasn't comfortable in my body. I have tried to seek help from my school's councillor and my friends for help, but their encouragement was not effective enough to bring me to a place of calmness and peace.

When you are sad and there's something inside you that makes you think irritational, act irritational, and believe that you're not worth it on earth. It's hard to listen to what people have to say to you on earth. I was completely consumed by the darkness and as I walked up the hill, I thought wow life's burden is so difficult all I could see is the shortcuts of life. I wanted to walk those shortcuts. At the end of walking the hill, I felt peace and it was the peace that come over and replenished me. God can do the same for you. I couldn't see the future. I was broken. What was I going to do in my life now? What's the point? Nothing in my life was going as I wanted it to.

Sharing my experience with you is to encourage you, and to show you what God has done for me He sure can do it for you. walking without the Lord God was scary I felt I was always alone, and my decision-making was not always fruitful because the Lord was not in it. from the time I made the Lord the head of my plans, then I saw the blessings and the wonders of God.

I know sharing my experience with you will help you on your journey You may be experiencing some awful moments in your life where you want to give up on everything in your marriage because you think you married the wrong person. That person is taking advantage of your goodness. They frustrate your plans you cannot even have a conversation because you are under pressure. Whenever you see that person you get anxious your hope for showing love is thin. You just want to end this marriage. I want you to take every burden to God. He sees and knows what you are going through. you know that you are not alone. There are others like you who are experiencing similar situations as you.

Christ will make the darkness within your heart that constantly covers you fall away. God that day, helped me. I wanted to give up, I wanted to turn my back and God and do my own thing. Being a cheerful, young woman with a horrible sense of wanting to have my own way, was not cool for me back then. So that's when I decided to ask God to participate. I was never like that, I knew Christ, and I knew about God. So why would I want to think like that? Why would I want to end my relationship with God so suddenly? I will tell you why, because I would constantly consume myself with stagnant thoughts, I allowed people to talk down on me, and I didn't want to believe that my life was worth it. But that day, I made that rash decision, to trust *Him*.

Chapter Twelve

How does God fight our battles?

Romans 8:31 says, "What then shall we say to these things? If God is for us, who can be against us?"

Muster your faith in God, He will help you when you feel that there is no hope. Isaiah 41: 10 says, "Fear not, for I am with you; be not dismayed, for I am your God; I will strengthen you, I will help you, I will uphold you with my righteous right hand."

Psalms 34: 17 says, "When the righteous cry for help, the Lord hears and delivers them out of all their troubles."

Isaiah 54:17 says, "No weapon that is fashioned against you shall succeed, and you shall confute every tongue that rises against you in judgment. This is the heritage of the servants of the Lord and their vindication from me, declares the Lord."

I want to remind you that God is for you, and He will fight your fights. God can get us through mental battles such as depression, and anxiety. If you are in the valley Don't you worry God will come down the valley and pick you up remember He came down on this earth to die for our sins to set us free. Also, maybe in the red light having no hope of seeing not even the amber light much less the green light, He will and is the one that will give you the go-ahead no matter if your lights are not working.

The Bible is there to show us God's love

I want to use the example, of Exodus, when God encouraged Moses to go and free the Israelites in Egypt. They had spent years under the oppression of Pharaoh. They were the slaves of Egypt. God saw that they were in pain, and He physically chose Moses to deliver them.

Isaiah 42: 13 says "The Lord goes out like a mighty man, like a man of war he stirs up his zeal; he cries out, He shouts aloud, He shows Himself mighty against His foes."

The Lord makes a promise to us, in Isaiah 43:2 says, "When you pass through the waters, I will be with you; and through the rivers, they shall not overwhelm you; when you walk through fire you shall not be burned, and the flame shall not consume you."

Luke 10: 19 says, "Behold, I have given you authority to tread on serpents and scorpions, and over all the power of the enemy, and nothing shall hurt you."

God has made a promise that with any situation you're in, the battle you're facing, no matter how big or small, He will always be present. Exodus 14:14 (ESV) says that "The Lord will fight for you, and you have only to be silent." Look, how amazing God is, you don't need to take part in your battles, God literally has promised us, is to stand still and watch Him do the wonders.

Deuteronomy 3:22, God makes a promise to us, "for it is the Lord who fights for you". Do you feel the power in those words? In this promise? All you need to do is ask God to take over. If you're struggling to pray to Him, below is a small prayer for you.

Dear Lord God,

You can see how much trouble I am facing, I feel like my life is crumbling before my eyes, (my problem – speak out your problem) and is tearing me apart Lord. I can't participate in society in the way I wish to, I can't enjoy life. I don't know how.

Lord, I want you to heal me, and purify me so I can see you clearly. You said to the Israelites that you're the only one who can heal them in Exodus 15:26 "I am the LORD, the one who heals you." God, I recognise that my problem can only be solved by you.

My mind is weak Lord, my body is tired, I am tired. I just want things to change Lord, I want everything to change. I want a change in my life, a renewed life with you where I can see your light clearly in my life.

Lord here, I want to confess to you and ask you that I need your help. I am nothing without you. I cannot eat and think properly without you. Holy Spirit, I need you within me, I want you to be in my heart, Christ Jesus. I want you Lord, to play a part in my life, I want my life to be whole, I want to surrender my heart, my soul, and my life to you, Lord. I have messed up my life and Lord I am starting to see it now. I want you to create a revelation in my life. Clearly, I desire to demonstrate to others how good You have been to me. Christ please be merciful to me and answer this prayer. Please forgive me for my sins. In Jesus' name, I pray, Amen.

Chapter Thirteen

God's Love

I want us to remember that God's love is thought of as the most complex thing in the world but in truth, it isn't. It's just like how a parent grows to love their child, the love forms, but for God, He doesn't need to see us 'grow' to love us, He loves us from when we were in the stomach, Jeremiah 1: 5 (ESV) says "Before I formed you in the womb, I knew you, and before you were born, I consecrated you." You have to understand that with all people around the world, God loves us, His love is unexplainable and it's hard for us sinners to accept that.

In Lamentations 3: 22 (GNB) "The Lord's unfailing love and mercy still continue." God's love is unfailing, unfailing in the dictionary means without fail or fault. There might be a time in your life when you thought someone love you the same way that you loved them, they hurt you, and now you can't look at love the same way as you did before. God's love is different, it's patient. There were times when I walked away but God's love always accepted me when I came back.

God's love is constant a love which is worth more than any love in the world, God truly cuddles us in His love. God's love is as soft as a big teddy bear or as delicate as a daisy, His love is warm like a hot plate of food, and that's what His love feels like. It's even more than that, these are finite examples of who God truly is. Another true example of God's love is patience.

1st Corinthians 13: 4-8 (GNB) says "Love is patient and kind; it is not jealous or conceited or proud; Love is not ill-mannered or selfish or irritable; love does not keep a record of wrongs; love is not happy with evil but is happy with the truth." God's love is so amazing and freshening, his love is patient and kind. For all of your life, whilst you've been practicing by yourself, getting on with your life, God has been waiting for you, He's seen you when you were at your lowest, He has seen you when you were bankrupt, He saw you when your boyfriend dumped you, He was there when you got your license, He was there when you moved into your own apartment/house. God is always there, He is always present

A true testament to God's love was found in the death of His son Jesus. Before Jesus died and rose again, Jesus shared with us stories of how God is with us. At times, we don't want to believe in it, we state these parables as mere stories, but they aren't. They are the physical analogies of how God is with us. Christ showed us an example in His parable of the prodigal son (Luke 15:11-32). The story of the prodigal son shows us that our father (the prodigal son's father) will always welcome us with open arms, in fact,

He is more excited that you are deciding to come back to Him. In verse 27, the servant is talking to the brother, the prodigal son came home and the "father has killed the fattened calf because he has him back safe and sound." This is what God does for us when we come back to Him, He prepares the feasts in heaven. God is happy that you are taking the time to talk to Him. God has found you, and He wants you to talk to Him, right now. God is excited that you're back home, the angels are in celebration because you have let Him into your life

In the second part, it says, "Love never gives up; and its faith, hope, and patience never fail. Love is eternal." I want to tell you that the Lord never gives up, He has not given up on you. He's been waiting for you and it's time for you to take the chance with Him. That's all he wants. Psalms 86: 15 says "But you, O Lord, are a God merciful and gracious, slow to anger and abounding in steadfast love and faithfulness." Romans 5: 8 says "But God shows His love for us in that while we were still sinners, Christ died for us." God's love is eternal, just like His relationship with us.

Chapter Fourteen

How does God's love show in your life?

God is there for you and with you

Deuteronomy 6:5 (GNB) says "Love the LORD your God with all your heart, with all your soul, and with all your strength." This verse in the Bible showed you that God wants you to give Him your all. He will fight the obstacles in your way. His desire is to give you strength. Though your mountain may be big as you look ahead and think that there is no way out, trust in the Lord God with all your heart. The battle is not yours it is the Lord God. The devil might think that he has wrapped you like a boa constrictor (type of snake) and you cannot move. Be not afraid the master knows exactly what to do He will help you through it all.

God's Love

John 3: 16 (GNB) says "For God loved the world so much that he gave His only Son so that everyone who believes in him may not die but have eternal life." God gave us Christ, for all of us, including you. God's purpose is to save us all, to save because He loves us. He doesn't want you to give up now, He wants you to be steadfast in His love. He is the one who never lives the one behind. God's love is unconditional. It will never fail. His love is PERFECT. Don't be fooled to think that God doesn't care for you. God does care He cares for you. Matthew 1:18-19 (GNB) says "This was how the birth of Jesus Christ took place. His mother Mary was engaged to Joseph, but before they were married, she found out that she was going to have a baby through the Holy Spirit. Joseph was a man who always did what was right, but he did not want to disgrace Mary publicly; so, he made plans to break the engagement privately." Psalms 103: 12 (GNB) says "As far as the east is from the west, so far does he remove our sins from us."

God's Love is shown in testimony.

It is a season where so many things going on corvid19 is one of them it was and is a sad situation for many of us experienced losing a loved one. A time when so many people lose their job, and homes. It is a time where by I had to cope with the different changes of attending University, so many changes to accommodate the way how the university functions social distancing studies were resumed to online accessing library books, it was not as simple as going to the library a being in the library. Thanks to God I got my degree. Now that I have the degree but by so many jobs lost, I was wondering God I just got my degree what about the job I was reminded that God is the biggest recruiter and employer He will give me a job. The question I asked is, is there anything too hard for God? Jeremiah 32:27 *"Behold, I am the Lord, the*

God of all flesh: is there anything too hard for me?" Moving forward when I apply for jobs God gave me numerous offers that reminded me He is real and powerful. I now have a job and I praise God for his goodness and kindness.

How can God's love show in your life?

1 John 4:16 says "And so we know and rely on the love God has for us. God is love. Whoever lives in love lives in God, and God in them."

Just like Job, our life can be changed, there is nothing in the world that God can't do.

Romans 8: 1 (GNB) says "There is no condemnation now for those who live in union with Christ Jesus." These Bible verses remind us that God's love is sweet, and He is willing to give us his love. Don't be afraid to seek His love.

Chapter Fifteen

The Pain of Losing a Baby

The pain of losing a baby is detrimental to anybody wanting to have a baby. Wow, wow where do I begin? So painful. Many women without a shadow of a doubt have experienced such heartbroken moments. Moments of full-on tears. I mean unstoppable tears. This type of tear you want no one to wipe because you feel at that moment you have let yourself down. The moment when you feel the whole world against you and you begin to think you are not worth it, the one thing you want to happen to you is losing your baby. As a result, you begin to say *"why "I should have" I could have."*

You begin to build a web of guilt around you. eventually becoming a chain that you cannot break. Thinking that there might not be another chance of having a baby. Not only that you do not want to try again because you don't want to end up having that same brokenness. With that thoughts, you begin to shut the windows and doors of your heart. Not letting anyone in and the blame and hatred games begin.

You start by thinking that God did not answer your prayers He does not love you anymore. Especially when you feel like you have devoted your life to Him, you married, you basically followed the rules that God has set, and you lose that baby, and you are like *"God where are you?" are you there? "Are you listening? "Do you really care"* saying those words come with discontent because you are literally angry with God. Prayer for you starts to become secondary the feeling and communication between you and God are becoming distant. Resentment is becoming a thing you are harvesting because at that moment you think you lost everything.

Well, when I lost my baby I was angry with God, because I desperately wanted a baby. I went into a deep sadness I was only in my early twenties. I remember some people saying to me you will have more babies you are only young. *"I was like hell no I want a baby now!"* I was angry terribly angry with myself and God. *I remember saying to God please do not call me. I do not want to hear you; you do not love me as you say.* I fail to read my Bible I felt like I was in a big cage all chained up and I cannot come out of it because I was just sad and angry that God did not save my baby.

For me, I thought God with His power could not help me. But someone reminded me that God loves me even if the baby was not saved but at least He saved my fallopian tubes so there is another chance of having a baby. That very moment I felt a peace come up to me I saw the light shine in my deepest corner. I went down on my knees talking to God I felt He embrace me. He said my child even in your mother's womb I knew you I shape you. I know you were angry, and it is okay but the one thing I am proud of you is that you pause and listen to what I had to say. Ladies, it is sad losing a baby, but God will bless you don't give up on Him you may have not one, but several miscarriages and you feel like you want to give up you don't even want to talk to God because you have hurt too many times, wait for God. Trust in His promise it shall come to pass don't give up, God doesn't want you to anyway He wants to make miracles for you and make you great because He is great.

To finish my testimony God bless me with three beautiful children my relationship with God takes the best turn because God showed me no matter when things go wrong if I put my trust in Him any chain that is holding me down, He will break every chain. God is the God in the mountain, and He is the God in the valley. Isaiah 61:3 "…to grant to those who mourn in Zion— to give them a beautiful headdress instead of ashes, the oil of gladness instead of mourning, the garment of praise instead of a faint spirit; that they may be called oaks of righteousness, the planting of the Lord, that he may be glorified." Corinthians 1:5 "For as we share abundantly in Christ's sufferings, so through Christ we share abundantly in comfort too."

This is one of my top verses because it reminds me that Christ suffered the ultimate punishment for our sins while dying on the cross and that we will also share his suffering as well. However, even though we will endure pain and loss in this life, we also will share in His comfort. The apostle Paul goes on to write in 2

Corinthians 13:11, *"Finally, brothers, rejoice. Aim for restoration, comfort one another, agree with one another, live in peace; and the God of love and peace will be with you."* This verse speaks to me about how we can also encourage and console one another as well. Do not let the pain and bruise of losing your baby form chains that you cannot move to talk to God. Give Him your all let go and let God take over. Call on his name with a loud shout demons tremble at the sound of His name. I know losing a child may not be replaceable for some people. Clearly, it is nothing that one can say to ease the pain or even lessen the pain of the person who is suffering the loss of their child only God's love can bring peace. And His word is an effective tool for doing just that.

The Heavenly Father is not happy to see you when you are going through your addiction, yet He also understands the deepest pain you are going through. God will bring relief to your pain. God only can turn your pain into joy when your addiction is at its highest God will bring hope and profound peace to you. It may perhaps seem unfeasible for the intense sadness and pain you feel at the loss of a child to ever diminish or decrease; nevertheless, the Lord is your hope and maker. God wants to encourage you and relieve your suffering if you will just pray to Him and read His word in the Bible. And His word is powerful enough to bring healing and solace even during your sadness.

Chapter Sixteen

Overweight: Can be a Struggle

There are millions of people struggling or just stressed about being overweight. The frustration of being overweight turns into a stronghold because it becomes a battle to overcome. For some people being overweight could be due to medication. It could be for some the stress of life and everything that is going on in their life that is not workable so therefore food is the next thing they turn to.

And there are some people who just love food and it is hard for them to control when they do take a bite. I can relate to that I personally love food and that was a stronghold to fight. My sister Jonell could put her hands up and say Bess really loves food, especially growing up as a child. Confession! I used to take my sister's food on her plate. Food was not my best friend, but I love it that's all I can say. At some point in my life, I did manage to keep the weight down, but it was yet still a battle I try many diets which just did not work. I remember after having my son Abba I piled on so much weight I was frustrated I remember looking in the mirror and all I could see was that I was so overweight I cried in front of the mirror for an hour plus. The Holy Spirit reminded me, *"you, pray to God for everything, but you do not pray to God for your weight issues."* And sometimes we do, we are scared, or we think that certain things are irrelevant to talk to God about, God wants us to come to Him with every problem that we may have that is distracting our life and plummeting our relationship that we want to have with God.

As soon as I heard the message from the Holy Spirit I prayed to God and asked God to help me to be a lover of his word and not of food. I asked Him to arrest my appetite for food, give me the spirit of moderation, and show me a fitness exercise that I can follow so that I can lose weight. I did ask God to touch my metabolism, and let it work for my body not against it. I remember the Holy Spirit choosing Leslie Sansone's exercise 'Walk at Home.' I started on the 11th of June 2020 at 16 stone and for seven months now I am almost 12 stone. I am no longer a lover of food God has spoken the chains are falling. Jesus is there to break the chain, whatever causes your food trigger I want you to take your problems to God the father He will do the same for you. He did it for me and others He can surely do it for you. Do not give in to any thoughts that tell you that you are overweight and there is nothing you can do this is just a deception to have your minds think that it is impossible to lose weight.

I have people who said to me you will not lose the weight just accept that you are big bone. Praise be to God He talks me out of that foolishness. God wants to do the same and more to you just as he did for me. He breaks the chains and breaks them fast to set His children free from the bondage and of stronghold. God is the blacksmith that will melt your chains away and turn them into keys that will unlock doors for you that everyone who thought that the doors were not able to be open, opened. Being over-weight can cause so many discomforts to the body, there are so many stories of people who were stuck on rides on funfairs, and they were so embarrassed by it all. As a result, that has a good impact on some people to lose weight for some it has made their situation worse. I want to tell you if you have encountered such discomfort do not lose hope God is there to give you all the sup-port you need hold on and trust in His promises, they are real. He alone can fight the battles for you. I am not here to condemn and say that being overweight is a sin no it is not a sin. Gluttony is a sin because in Philippians 3: 19 said that some gods are their ap-petite they will just eat and that is all that matter to them. How-ever, the true God wants to change that of you. God wants his children to look after their bodies, our bodies are the temple of the Lord. Romans 12:1-2 "I appeal to you, therefore, brothers, by the mercies of God, to present your bodies as a living sacrifice, holy and acceptable to God, which is your spiritual worship. Do not be conformed to this world, but be transformed by the re-newal of your mind, that by testing you may discern what is the will of God, what is good and acceptable and perfect. His yearn-ing is to transport you to a path that will draw you closer to Him.

God Wants You to Eat Healthily.

God's desire is to bring you to perfection He wants you to exercise, and have self-control through being hearers and doers of His word. When you be obedient to what \God says you will never go wrong because His word will be a lamp onto your feet and a light unto your path as it said in Psalms 119: 105 *Thy word is a lamp unto my feet and a light unto my path.* When you eat the right foods which include vegetables, fruits, healthy proteins, and whole grains. God wants you to stay healthy He has fantastic plans for you on earth for you to do for Him. When you eat, He wants you to eat to be satisfied not to eat and you are so full up you want to vomit. Proverbs 25:16 *"If you have found honey, eat only enough for you, lest you have your fill of it and vomit it."* Look at the story of the children of Israel when they were emancipated from Egypt, they were given manner sent from heaven by God, however, most of them did not happy with that type of regime they wanted what they thought was real food the food that they use to in Egypt their complaint was so great, at that point God gives the food that they wanted, this does not say that God was lenient it shows that God does not govern people lives, but He gives them the power of choice. Bear in mind that God does not force anyone but admonishes you in the direction that will lead you to life eternal. I encourage whatever you do, do it for the glory of God. Some people may want to lose weight for so many reasons to fit into their marriage dress to find their dream job, or through intense pressure. Please don't get me wrong if that's the motivation go ahead. But when this dream has been fulfilled some start to slip back into their old ways of eating. And this just what happen to me I lose weight on occasions when I did meet those desires I fell back into my old habit of eating. Because I did not let the spirit of God lead me. Do not let people or the world pressure you, also do not let them have you compare yourself to others. When I was growing up people used to say to me *"why are you so fat and your sister so skinny, it was horrible to hear back then.* Thank God for my mother Tofa who mentored me through this difficult ordeal of people's mouths of having no consideration for others feeling. These are that lovely texts from the great book of the Bible. Philippians 4:8 Finally, brothers, whatever is true, whatever is honourable, whatever is just, whatever is pure, whatever is lovely, whatever is worthy, if there is any brilliance, if there is anything worthy of praise, think about these things. Ephesians 4:22-23 to put off your old self, which belongs to your former manner of life and is corrupt through untrustworthy desires, and to be renewed in the spirit of your minds. Romans 12:2 Do not be conformed to this present world, but be transformed by the rejuvenating of your mind, so that you may test and approve what is the will of God–what is good and well-pleasing and perfect. Hang on to those words it is an encouragement it is comforting words to digest.

My Healthy Regime

- Firstly, when I get up in the morning I pray to God,
- Next, I do about 100 minutes of exercise sometimes all at

once or I break the exercise into segments. That exercise is Leslie Sansone's 'Walk at Home' her 45 mins and 10 mins Cardio Blast.'

- I do 2 times 45 and 1 ten mins.
- Sometimes I just do 40 mins of the Cardio Blast each day except Saturday.
- I always invite God because I know His strength is perfect in helping me complete my daily routine.
- Start my breakfast with a fruit smoothie.
- By 12-30 pm I eat a big lunch
- For dinner I have something exceptionally light and water till when I am ready to sleep.

I have to take my eating habits to God, Remember that you can do all things through the Lord Jesus who strengthens you. Take God at His word and prove Him. He will remove any chains that blocking your path.. He will set you free.

Chapter Seventeen

Depression

Depression! Depression! many of us had a depressive episode in one way or another whether through clinical or diagnosis. Depression is not a very nice thing to experience, there a people who have no idea that they are suffering from depression because they haven't been taught about it. There are also people who suffer from depression, and they don't like to talk about it. Depression can be seen as a stigma in some cultures. For instance, if someone says they are depressed in some culture they will classify as having weak minds. Even so in the male environment, some men don't often talk of their depression for fear of being looked upon as weak. So, therefore, men who are depressed would suffer in silence until sometimes it is too late. The encouragement here is don't be afraid to seek help talk to a friend talk to God He will lead you to the right people. Don't be afraid you are not alone stretch your hands to God today, for God understands your pain. Depression can be a scary place to be, full of isolation. God can break the shackles of depression.

Depression could happen to anyone at any time, so many variables can trigger depression-like trauma, abuse, bereavement, etc. A person who suffers from depression is easy to feel hopeless and sometimes feels like nobody cares for them, and they rather be alone. The good news there is someone who cares and wants to break that chain of depression He wants to give you your life back. His name is Jesus Christ the son of God. He has been in the world before and has experienced what you have gone through or maybe still going through. Jesus is ever willing to break the chain for you. We are living in a world today where uncertainty seems like the norm and for many people, it is too much to handle. As a result, that leads to people becoming wearier and wanting to give up. Experiencing fear and anxiety and a range of feelings of hopelessness and sadness can cause many people to drop their interest in things that once made them happy. Depression may have a negative effect on your life, but God is ever so present to make you depression free.

If you want to not be afraid anymore the Bible talks about people who were depressed, and God helps them live without fear. Remember Job was despaired by losing all that he have his livelihood, his house, and his children.

Job in his depressive state

After this, Job opened his mouth and cursed the day of his birth. He said: "May the day of my birth perish, and the night that said, 'A boy is conceived!' That day—may it turn to darkness; may God above not care about it; may no light shine on it. May gloom and utter darkness claim it once more; may a cloud settle over it; may blackness overwhelm it. That night—may thick darkness seize it; may it not be included among the days of the year nor be entered in any of the months. May that night be barren; may no shout of joy be heard in it.

May those who curse days curse that day, those who are ready to rouse Leviathan. May its morning stars become dark; may it wait for daylight in vain and not see the first rays of dawn, for it did not shut the doors of the womb on me to hide trouble from my eyes. "Why did I not perish at birth, and die as I came from the womb? Why were there knees to receive me and breasts that I might be nursed? For now, I would be lying down in peace; I would be asleep and at rest with kings and rulers of the earth, who built for themselves places now lying-in ruins, with princes who had gold, who filled their houses with silver. Or why was I not hidden away in the ground like a stillborn child, like an infant who never saw the light of day? There is the wicked ceases from turmoil, and there the weary are at rest. Captives also enjoy their ease; they no longer hear the slave driver's shout. The small and the great are there, and the slaves are freed from their owners. "Why is light given to those in misery, and life to the bitter of soul, to those who long for death that does not come, who search for it more than for hidden treasure, who are filled with gladness and rejoice when they reach the grave? Why is life given to a man whose way is hidden, whom God has hedged in? For sighing has become my daily food; my groans pour out like water. What I feared has come upon me; what I dreaded has happened to me. I have no peace, no quietness; I have no rest, but only turmoil.

It is not Job alone in the Bible who experiences depression, the Bible presents many more stories of depressed individuals pleading for God's assistance time after time. Depression is a stronghold that God is willing to break for his children. God has helped Job, Jonah, Jeremiah, and Elijah He can do the same for you.

Jonah in his depressive state

Jonah another prophet of God was so depressed because he did not want to go to Nineveh. He run away from God, or I would say he try to run away from Him because no one can run away from God anyway.

Jonah's Anger at the Lord's Compassion

But to Jonah, this seemed very wrong, and he became angry. He prayed to the Lord, "Isn't this what I said, Lord when I was still at home? That is what I tried to forestall by fleeing to Tarshish. I knew that you are a gracious and compassionate God, slow to anger and abounding in love, a God who relents from sending calamity. Now, Lord, take away my life, for it is better for me to die than to live." But the Lord replied, "Is it right for you to be angry?" Jonah had gone out and sat down at a place east of the city. There he made himself a shelter, sat in its shade, and waited to see what would happen to the city. Then the Lord God provided a leafy plant and made it grow up over Jonah to give shade for his head to ease his discomfort, and Jonah was very happy about the plant. But at dawn the next day God provided a worm, which chewed the plant so that it withered. When the sun rose, God provided a scorching east wind, and the sun blazed on Jonah's head so that he grew faint. He wanted to die, and said, "It would be better for me to die than to live." But God said to Jonah, "Is it right for you to be angry about the plant?" "It is," he said. "And I'm so angry I wish I were dead. But the Lord said, You have been concerned about this plant, though you did not tend it or make it grow. It sprang up overnight and died overnight. And should I not have concern for the great city of Nineveh, in which there are more than a hundred and twenty thousand people who cannot tell their right hand from their left—and also many animals?"

Other people in the Bible like Elijah gain huge exposure against the prophet of Baal, yet Elijah fled from Jezebel and was so depressed He asked God to take his life. However, God did not take Elijah's life but encouraged him to go be steadfast in his word and heal Elijah, Jonah, Job, and all others breaking the chains of depression. It is obvious that depression is a chain that roped the minds of people. put them in a state of destitution and remoteness failing to mingle. In constant struggle mostly every day.

Jeremiah

Jeremiah a prophet was struggling with depression during the course of his life. He was so heavily depressed like Job he curse the day that he was born or come to earth. He was denied and ridiculed by his own people. Yet the lord God was able to use Jeremiah and help with his depression. God was not going to stand and see his prophets suffer at the hands of Satan. God will take charge and save you just as He did for others. You need to be willing and let God work for you. Don't let go of God's His will is to always be on your side to help you. Remember depression is a real persistent problem, that God wants to solve for you breaking the chain of your mountain.

Some Signs of Depression

- Tearful, restless guilty
- worthless and down on yourself
- Unfilled and numb isolated and unable to relate to other people.
- A sense of unreality and no self-confidence or self-esteem
- Hopeless and despairing and suicidal.

No matter what the difficulties that come with depression God is ever willing to break the chains. Jesus recognized and understood the pain and He knows the chain is heavy to carry He said in Matthew 11: 28-30"Come to me, all you who are weary and burdened, and I will give you rest. Take my yoke upon you and learn from me, for I am gentle and humble in heart, and you will find rest for your souls. For my yoke is easy and my burden is light."

Chapter Eighteen

Secret Deception

Deception is the practice of misleading, telling a constant lie and keeping a secret. It is not mainly about telling lies deception can comprise falsifying the truth and so many misrepresentations of good. When a person does things that are not right is a form of deception. Deception is a stronghold and God hates it because people are rub of the blessings of God. God's desire is to break the chain of deception from your life. He doesn't want you to keep these lies a secret He wants to bring your secret lies out from you and set you free once and for all. Let's hear what the Bible says about deception before moving on, first of all, deception is consist of lies in Proverbs 12:22 "Lying lips are an abomination to the Lord, but those who act faithfully are his delight." *Galatians 6:7-8* "Do not be deceived: God is not mocked, for whatever one sows, that will he also reap. For the one who sows to his own flesh will from the flesh reap corruption, but the one who sows to the Spirit will from the Spirit reap eternal life." **Proverbs 10:9** "Whoever walks in integrity walks securely, but he who makes his ways crooked will be found out."

Deception is a Trap

There are secrets people don't want to share because they think that if they share that secret it might land them in trouble, sometime that may be the case. Another thing why people won't share is because they may think that they will look upon as a lesser person depending on the circumstances that they find themselves in. Some of the deceptive life can be seen as a person having affairs and thinking that they will never get caught and telling lies to cover up their untruthfulness. But there is the man name Jesus with whom you can share your secret He alone can set you free of deception. You might think you are obligated to keep your secret and do your own thing but there are consequences for every action. God wants to save you from those situations. The devil puts deception in your way as his strategy to trap you from the blessings of the Lord God. Look at the story of Ananias and his wife Sapphira they were living a deceptive life lying to cover up deceitful behaviours unfortunately, they were so heavily trapped in the deception they fail to bring it to the Lord God. You will see the full story in Acts 5:1-11.

Another story of Samson a Nazarite in the book of Judges who were not allowed to trim his hair nor drink strong drink. Samson had immense power given to him by God. He was so embedded by God with this enormous intensity, which he used to fight the Philistines who were always at war with the Israelites. But one day Samson got involved with a woman named Delilah. A woman who was full of deception a woman that God did not desire for Samson. However, Samson decided to pursue Delilah but Delilah with her deceptive motives had trapped Samson and therefore Samson was enticed into her trap. It was a complicated ending to Samson's outcome.

Samson Story: Judges 14.

And Samson went down to Timnath and saw a woman in Timnath of the daughters of the Philistines. And he came up, and told his father and his mother, and said, I have seen a woman in Timnath of the daughters of the Philistines: now, therefore, get her for me to wife. Then his father and his mother said unto him, Is there never a woman among the daughters of thy brethren, or among all my people, that thou goes to take a wife of the uncircumcised Philistines? And Samson said unto his father, Get her for me; for she pleases me well. But his father and his mother knew not that it was of the Lord, that he sought an occasion against the Philistines: for at that time the Philistines had dominion over Israel. Then went Samson down, and his father and his mother, to Timnath, and came to the vineyards of Timnath: and behold, a young lion roared against him. And the Spirit of the Lord came mightily upon him, and he rent him as he would have rent a kid, and he had nothing in his hand: but he told not his father or his mother what he had done. And he went down and talked with the woman, and she pleased Samson well. And after a time, he returned to take her, and he turned aside to see the carcass of the lion: and behold, there was a swarm of bees and honey in the carcass of the lion. And he took thereof in his hands, and went on eating, and came to his father and mother, and he gave them, and they did eat but he told not them that he had taken the honey out of the carcass of the lion. So, his father went down unto the woman: and Samson made there a feast; for so used the young men to do. And it came to pass, when they saw him, that they brought thirty companions to be with him. And Samson said unto them, I will now put forth a riddle unto you: if ye can certainly declare it me within the seven days of the feast, and find it out, then I will give you thirty sheets and thirty change of garments: But if ye cannot declare it me, then shall ye give me thirty sheets and thirty change of garments. And they said unto him, Put forth thy riddle, that we may hear it. And he said unto them, Out of the eater came forth meat, and out of the strong came forth sweetness. And they could not in three days expound the riddle. And it came to pass on the seventh day, that they said unto Samson's wife, Entice thy husband, that he may declare unto us the riddle, lest we burn thee and thy father's house with fire: have ye called us to take that we have? is it not so? And Samson's wife wept before him, and said, Thou dost but hate me, and loves me not: thou hast put forth a riddle unto the children of my people, and hast not told it to me. And he said unto her, Behold, I have not told it my father nor my mother, and shall I tell it thee? And she wept before him the seven days, while their feast lasted: and it came to pass on the seventh day, that he told her because she lay sore upon him: and she told the riddle to the children of her people. And the men of the city said unto him on the seventh day before the sun went down, What is sweeter than honey? And what is stronger than a lion? and he said unto them, If ye had not ploughed with my heifer, ye had not found out my riddle. And the Spirit of the Lord came upon him, and he went down to Ashkelon, and slew thirty men of them, and took their spoil, and gave change of garments unto them which expounded the riddle. And his anger was kindled, and he went up to his father's house. But Samson's wife was given to his companion, whom he had used as his friend."

Only God can Judge you
Matthew 7:1-5

"Judge not, that you be not judged. For with the judgment, you pronounce you will be judged, and with the measure, you use it will be measured to you. Why do you see the speck that is in your brother's eye, but not notice the log that is in your own eye? Or how can you say to your brother, 'Let me take the speck out of your eye,' when there is the log in your own eye? You hypocrite first take the log out of your own eye, and then you will see clearly to take the speck out of your brother's eye.

I am not here to Judge you only God is the judge. And He will Judge whom He has to Judge accordingly. God's focus is to break down every chain in your life. God can turn things around to give you that blessed hope that you don't feel the need to lie and cheat.

God will take you to a place where you so want to be. Life can be hard or troublesome when you are in a position where you cannot see where the help is going to come from trust in Jesus don't be afraid to come to Him because you feel guilty. God is waiting with arms wide open to transform you.

Chapter Nineteen

What if fornication is the stronghold

Fornication is a topic that sometimes pops up in a debate. Pastors preach extensively on the subject, and the Bible tells us it's against God's will to have sex outside of marriage. Fornication is the sin of pre-marital sex, it also involves those living together outside the union marriage. God warns that our body is His temple and wants us to stay away from the things that will defile our bodies. God created sex for us to enjoy but within the bounds of marriage.

God tells us in *1 Corinthians 6:18-20*, "to flee from sexual immorality. Every other sin a person commits is outside the body, but the sexually immoral person sins against his own body. Or do you not know that your body is a temple of the Holy Spirit within you, whom you have from God? You are not your own, for you were bought with a price. So, glorify God in your body." For some people, it might be difficult to abstain from fornication especially when you have been cohabiting for so long it becomes difficult to let go. For you, sex becomes pleasurable and routine. Sex outside of marriage can lead to unplanned and painful consequences. Sex was created by God for marriage only. The Bible clearly mentions all sexual relationships outside God's instruction are totally wrong. God is a God of principles and we got to adhere to His vision and mission for us. Some people might not want to believe in His word, but His word always stands the test. If you are in a relationship and you are not married, God wants you to hearken to His instructions, remember there are blessings attached to obedience. God is there to break the chains that stifle you, He can break those heavy chains that you think cannot be broken. **1 Corinthians 7:1-40 says,** "Now concerning the matters about which you wrote: "It is good for a man not to have sexual relations with a woman." But because of the temptation to sexual immorality, each man should have his own wife and each woman her own husband. The husband should give his wife her conjugal rights, and likewise the wife to her husband. The wife does not have authority over her own body, but the husband does. Likewise, the husband does not have authority over his own body, but the wife does. Do not deprive one another, except perhaps by agreement for a limited time, that you may devote yourselves to prayer; but then come together again, so that Satan may not tempt you because of your lack of self-control. You might be tempted and carry on with your life, **1 Corinthians 10:13** says, "No temptation has overtaken you that is not common to man. God is faithful, and He will not let you be tempted beyond your ability, but with the temptation, he will also provide the way of escape, that you may be able to endure it." I encourage you to let God direct your life and order your steps. Remember **1 Thessalonians 4:3-5 says,** "For this is the will of God, your sanctification: that you abstain from sexual immorality; that each one of you knows how to control his own body in holiness and honour, not in the passion of lust like the Gentiles who do not know God; Paul reminded the people at the brethren in his letter asking them to do not be imitated by the world. Do what is good and acceptable to the Lord God.

A testimony of how Jesus breakdown a strong hold on a woman's life

In the book of **John chapter 4: 7-25**, Jesus is challenged by a crowd of Jews who brought to Him a woman caught in the act of adultery. The people were eager for Jesus to give this young woman some form of public humiliation because they knew what she did was clearly a sin, and against the laws. So, she should be punished and stoned as prescribed by Mosaic Law. Not only that the people wanted to trap Jesus in what He thought of the woman. John 8:6-11 "They were trying to trap him into saying something they could use against him, but Jesus stooped down and wrote in the dust with his finger. They kept demanding an answer, so he stood up again and said, "All right, but let the one who has never sinned throw the first stone!" Then he stooped down again and wrote in the dust. When the accusers heard this, they slipped away one by one, beginning with the oldest, until only Jesus was left in the middle of the crowd with the woman. Then Jesus stood up again and said to the woman, "Where are your accusers? Didn't even one of them condemn you?"

"No, Lord," she said.

And Jesus said, "Neither do I. Go and sin no more." Jesus did not act like the people who condemn the woman. But save her from her sins and her addiction. Jesus will do the same for you in whatever situation you may find yourself in. Fornication doesn't bring true joy. Whenever we are ready for Jesus' help, He will gladly help us.

God is keeping it Real: Ephesians 5:1-20

"Be ye, therefore, followers of God, as dear children;

"And walk in love, as Christ also hath loved us, and hath given himself for us an offering and a sacrifice to God for a sweet-smelling savour. "But fornication, and all uncleanness, or covetousness, let it not be once named among you, as becometh saints; Neither filthiness, nor foolish talking, nor jesting, which are not convenient: but rather giving of thanks. For this ye know, that no whoremonger, nor unclean person, nor covetous man, who is an idolater, hath any inheritance in the kingdom of Christ and of God. Let no man deceive you with vain words: for because of these things cometh the wrath of God upon the children of disobedience. Be not ye, therefore, partakers with them. For ye were sometimes darkness, but now are ye light in the Lord: walk as children of light: (For the fruit of the Spirit is in all goodness and righteousness and truth;) Proving what is acceptable unto the Lord. And have no fellowship with the unfruitful works of darkness, but rather reprove them. For it is a shame even to speak of those things which are done of them in secret. But all things that are reproved are made manifest by the light: for whatsoever doth make manifest is light. Wherefore he saith, 'Awake thou that sleepiest, and arise from the dead, and Christ shall give thee light.' See then that ye walk circumspectly, not as fools, but as wise. Redeeming the time because the days are evil. Wherefore be ye not unwise but understanding what the will of the Lord is. And be not drunk with wine, wherein is excess; but be filled with the Spirit; speaking to yourselves in psalms and hymns and spiritual songs, singing and making melody in your heart to the Lord; Giving thanks always for all things unto God and the Father in the name of our Lord Jesus Christ."

God teaching for the home: Ephesians 5:21-33

"Submitting yourselves one to another in the fear of God. Wives, submit yourselves unto your own husbands, as unto the Lord. For the husband is the head of the wife, even as Christ is the head of the church: and he is the saviour of the body. Therefore, as the church is subject unto Christ, so let the wives be to their own husbands in everything.

"Husbands, love your wives, even as Christ also loved the church, and gave himself for it; That he might sanctify and cleanse it with the washing of water by the word, That he might present it to himself a glorious church, not having spot, or wrinkle, or any such thing; but that it should be holy and without blemish. So, ought men to love their wives as their own bodies? "He that loveth his wife loveth himself. For no man ever yet hated his own flesh; but nourisheth and cherisheth it, even as the Lord the church: For we are members of his body, of his flesh, and of his bones. For this, the cause shall a man leave his father and mother and shall be joined unto his wife, and they two shall be one flesh. This is a great mystery: but I speak concerning Christ and the church. Nevertheless, let every one of you in particular so love his wife even as himself; and the wife see that she reverences her husband."

Chapter Twenty

Unforgiving Spirit

When people get hurt the first thing they tend to do is to move away from the person that hurt them. For them, that person should go to hell for causing them pain. The person might have taken your money, said untruthful things about you, or disrupted your marital life causing you a lot of anxiety. Sometimes, you can't even forgive yourself because you have done something you deeply regret. When people experience such situations it can make their lives miserable and difficult to forgive themselves and others. No matter what counselling they receive, it still makes no difference because that hurt, or pain has taken root in the heart of the individual. Unforgiveness becomes a stronghold, and it only takes God's power to emancipate you from that mindset.

It is understandable that you are in pain with hurt from that betrayal but when you hold on to things in your heart it produces resentment and hate. God cannot hear a prayer of an unforgiving heart. Unforgiveness never hurts the other person. It only hurts you.

The Parable of the Unmerciful Servant

Then Peter came to Jesus and asked, "Lord, how many times shall I forgive my brother or sister who sins against me? Up to seven times?" Jesus answered, "I tell you, not seven times, but seventy-seven times. "Therefore, the kingdom of heaven is like a king who wanted to settle accounts with his servants. As he began the settlement, a man who owed him ten thousand bags of gold was brought to him. Since he was not able to pay, the master ordered that he and his wife and his children and all that he had be sold to repay the debt. "At this, the servant fell on his knees before him. 'Be patient with me,' he begged, 'and I will pay back everything.' The servant's master took pity on him, cancelled the debt, and let him go. "But when that servant went out, he found one of his fellow servants who owed him a hundred silver coins. He grabbed him and began to choke him. 'Pay back what you owe me!' he demanded. "His fellow servant fell to his knees and begged him, 'Be patient with me, and I will pay it back.' "But he refused. Instead, he went off and had the man thrown into prison until he could pay the debt. When the other servants saw what had happened, they were outraged and went and told their master everything that had happened. "Then the master called the servant in. 'You wicked servant,' he said, 'I cancelled all that debt of yours because you begged me to. Shouldn't you have had mercy on your fellow servant just as I had on you?' In anger, his master handed him over to the jailers to be tortured until he should pay back all he owed. "This is how my heavenly Father will treat each of you unless you forgive your brother or sister from your heart."

What does the Bible say?

Matthew 18:21-22, "Then Peter came to Jesus and said, 'Lord, how many times may my brother sin against me, and I forgive him, up to seven times?' Jesus said to him, 'I tell you, not seven times but seventy times seven!'"

Leviticus 19:17-18, "Do not bear a grudge against others, but settle your differences with them, so that you will not commit a sin because of them. Do not take revenge on others or continue to hate them but love your neighbours as you love yourself. I am the Lord."

Mark 11:25, "And when you stand and pray, forgive anything you may have against anyone so that your Father in heaven will forgive the wrongs you have done."

Matthew 5:23-24, "So if you are about to offer your gift to God at the altar and there you remember that your brother has something against you, leave your gift there in front of the altar, go at once and make peace with your brother, and then come back and offer your gift to God."

Matthew 6:14-15, "For if you forgive others their sins, your heavenly Father will also forgive you. But if you do not forgive others, your Father will not forgive you your sins."

Chapter Twenty-one

Pride

Pride, for many, is a stronghold. A battle that none can really fight off, it only takes the force of God to do so. If you humble yourself before the Lord and obey His laws and ethics, you will receive the blessings that He has in store for you. God despises the sin of pride, and He will humble those who are prideful. Pride has caused many to remain behind because they thought they can do it all by themselves or that they know it all. Having these types of prideful behaviours won't elevate you, and certainly won't take you anywhere. Look at Satan, his pride and vanity cost him his place in heaven. From God's favourite angel, he became the reproach of the universe. Pride is a slow, silent killer, it takes people from grace to grass. Satan refused to surrender to God, he wanted to be God. His pride and ego told him asking God for forgiveness would lower him. But God would have forgiven Satan if only he would have put pride aside and let God have His way in his life. But no, Satan refused and tried to cause havoc in heaven, and was cast out. Satan is a prideful deceiver, and after losing his place in heaven, his hobby became stealing, killing, and destroying. Satan doesn't have anything good to offer, and those who follow his prideful ways will ultimately fall down.

Isaiah 14:12-14 talks about Satan's prideful heart

"How art thou has fallen from heaven, O Lucifer, son of the morning! How art thou cut down to the ground, which didst weakens the nations! For thou hast said in thine heart, I will ascend into heaven, I will exalt my throne above the stars of God: I will sit also upon the mount of the congregation, in the sides of the north: I will ascend above the heights of the clouds; I will be like the Most High God. Yet thou shalt be brought down to hell, to the sides of the pit." Satan was not the only one to exhibit pride from the beginning, Adam and Eve also showed pride by yielding to Satan's deception to "be as wise as God". How wrong they were. They were so prideful they hid from God. Who can hide from God? Absolutely no one! God is the greatest and will always be. He is an awesome God.

Eve and Adam's Prideful Behaviour

In Genesis 3:4 – 6, we see that it is the sin of pride that caused Eve to eat of the forbidden fruit. "Then the serpent said to the woman, "You will not surely die. For God knows that in the day you eat of it your eyes will be opened, and you will be like God, knowing good and evil." So, when the woman saw that the tree was good for food, that it was pleasant to the eyes, and a tree desirable to make one wise, she took of its fruit and ate. She also gave it to her husband who was with her and ate it (Genesis 3:4 – 6)."

The Bible verses from different books about pride

Pride as we know is a barrier that prevents one from having a true relationship with God. When a person takes on pride, they rely on their own strength and become boastful. Everything has to be centred on themselves alone and God hates that attitude. Here is what the Bible says about pride: "To fear the Lord is to hate evil; I hate pride and arrogance, evil behaviour and perverse speech." And the Bible is quick to add that, "Pride goes before destruction, a haughty spirit before a fall." (Proverbs 8:13; 16:18). The heavenly father reminds us that pride is one of the issues that complicate our lives.

1 Corinthians 10:12 warns, "So, if you think you are standing firm, be careful that you don't fall!" wow this text is food for thought, please read it again, God's word is powerful. pride has caused us to become self-centred.

James 4:6, "Therefore, it says, 'God opposes the proud, but gives grace to the humble".

Luke 14:11 "For everyone who exalts himself will be humbled, and the one who humbles himself will be exalted".**1 Peter 5:5-7** "God resists the proud but gives grace to the humble. Humble yourselves, therefore, under the mighty hand of God, so that He may lift you up at the proper time, casting all your care on Him because He cares about you."

Pride (ego) is not a good ingredient in your recipe for life

Several years ago, when I got my first job, I was so excited and overjoyed that I forgot the One who made it possible for me to get the job. Jesus made the job possible, but I was carrying on as though I did it myself. Failing to recognize that all good things come from the Lord is a prideful attitude. God is the mastermind behind all good things and the glory must go to Him. Sometimes in life, you may go on thinking it is your own work that gets you where you are, but that is not totally true. Everything you've ever had, God gave you the wits and strength to acquire it. There is nothing wrong with being proud of your hard work. Just like there isn't anything wrong with being proud of having your home or having what you so desire. In fact, we're supposed to take pride in these things — to an extent. In Proverbs 12:27, the Bible says, "Inspires us to work hard so we'll be satisfied with the results. It says, "The diligent man prizes his possessions." We only commit the sin of pride when we take up self-glorification instead of thanking God for His kindness and generosity. Sinful pride is downplaying God's efforts.

The message here is to understand that when we take on an attitude to put ourselves first and not the creator who has created all things including you, it becomes pride. This type of pride will lead you to destruction. That pride will diminish you. Let's go back to Satan's folly, when God created him God gave him everything; beauty, a melodic voice, and wit. His name was called

Lucifer meaning son of the morning star. However, Satan allowed his beauty from God to puff up his ego and water the seeds of pride which later turned to the envy of God! Instead of confessing the behaviour and taking it to the Creator who had the power to destroy strongholds, Satan chose to stay in his mess.

When your mountain looms large and overwhelming, call on the name of the Lord. Lift up your voice and ask for help in the name of Jesus, don't be scared to ask for help, there is power in the name of Jesus – and the heavenly Father has given you access to it. Take those burdens to Him, drop them at His feet. Purge yourself of pride and humble yourself before the Lord.

Chapter Twenty-two

What if that Chain is your Marriage?

Marriage is an institution ordained by God. It is a system of pro-creation created for a husband and wife, in holy matrimony. A man and woman usually enter into marriage because they love each other, and want to sanctify their union. Marriage is not always a bed of roses. Meaning it is not always a fairy tale. Partners can make mistakes, make poor decisions, and sometimes get into arguments. These arguments may be small or big, but they are common occurrences. It is an everyday challenge for many people. However, the burden of marriage can become intolerable when two people go into marriage prematurely. In addition, a lack of intimacy is a recipe for marital breakdown. Marital issues such as unfaithfulness and abusiveness may start coming up. These chains in the marriage as mentioned can become so tangled that neither of the couples has a clue how to save their marriage. It's at this point that separation or divorce seemingly looks like a solution. Some of you may have children involved. And we know that children are the broken pieces when the home fall apart, they too are left with a heavy negative impact and sometimes find themselves repeating the same pattern. Marriage is not a chain, it is the negativity that occurs in a marriage that becomes chains, and many are scared to leave the toxic environment because of their children. They are scared that a divorce will negatively affect their children.

There are marriages where the wives or husbands have no say in the finance. Every transaction is closely monitored, and there is no togetherness in finance. This can be downright depressing and the solution is remaining silent hoping that there will be a change, or the chain will be broken. Well, the chain cannot be broken if you don't seek help to be free. That help can only come from God, remember marriage is His institution, and only He can fix it for you. Run to His bosom with your troubles. It doesn't matter if you sought God before your marriage or not, there is still room for deliverance. Bring your burdens before the Lord.

I know it might be difficult, especially if one partner is refusing to seek help from the Lord. But you must keep your hope and faith alive, there are no chains that God cannot break. No storm Jesus cannot calm, and no situation He cannot fix. He will fix your marriage. You may be newly married, and you'd thought the person you married was a prince or princess. He or she might have ticked all the perfect boxes on your checklist, only for you to get married and discover that the person you are married to is a wolf in sheep's clothing. You may be starting to realize you are married to a bully, an insecure person, or a controller, and there is nothing you can say or do that is right for them. Your family members can't even come by to see you. You have no say in anything. Psalm 55:22 says, "Cast your burden upon the Lord and He will sustain you; He will never allow the righteous to be shaken". Be prepared to give the chain to Lord. Marriage is beautiful when it passes through the spiritual conveyer belt. When marriage passes through the Creator of marriage, although it may seem to fall, it shall surely stand. Because God's thought toward His children is always good. Proverb 3:5 "Trust in the LORD with all your heart, and lean not on your own understanding; in all your ways acknowledge him, and he will make your paths straight". Psalms 37:5 says, "Commit your way to the LORD; trust in Him, and He will do it." "He who trusts in himself is a fool, but one who walks in wisdom will be safe (Proverbs 28:26)." God wants us to be wise by trusting Him. His plan is to smash the chains that hold us down and set us free. Be strong and of good courage. you are not alone in the fight against breaking chains. I encourage you to pray, it is the best form of communication between you and God, and it works tremendously. If you are reading this chapter and you are not married don't be put off, marriage is God's institution and God will always do His best to save what He created. So, whatever you do put Him first to guide you in making decisions.

Chapter Twenty-three

The Confession

What is my addiction? How can I come to terms with it? Is my addiction bigger than I am? These are the questions that everyone who has fought addiction thinks about. I would like you to write down what you want from this book.

What is your addiction?

An addiction can be anything that dominates or controls your everyday life. You just cannot do without that fix. It's like your little god you just can't say no to. It is a stronghold. It messes up people's minds when they fall victim to such conditions. Anyone suffering from addiction should seek help. It's not something you can fight on your own, you need help.

How are you fighting against it?

The fight against addictions is not a one-man's job. You need intervention, and the intervention is from the Holy Spirit. Only He can supply you with the strength, and courage to wrestle with your addiction. My addiction was food. My siblings would tell me I love food when I was growing up. So, I always had a battle with my teen weight. I thought I could fight my food battle on my own, but it took the love of Jesus to emancipate me. He can do the same for you and set you free.

How are you feeling once you do it?

Some people sometimes deny the fact that they are addicted. Even if they feel bad or look bad they will say they are okay when asked. Anyone who struggles with addiction usually feels powerless and helpless. But the good news is that you don't have to stay stuck in that terrible lane, you can switch lanes! And position yourself towards the master's lane, Jesus' lane. He will help fight your battles.

How do you want God to change you? What would you like from this book?

This is where you express your feelings to God and ask Him to help you with your addiction. I would suggest you start with a prayer. Next, write down what you want God to do for you, and finally, believe that He will come through for you.

What if I can't do it? What if I can't stop?

I want to tell you right now that you can stop, nothing is impossible with God. His grace makes things possible for us. With Him, we can do the extraordinary. When I was battling with my addictions, I thought the same thing – how was I going to steadily stop my addiction? Will it ever stop? I thought about it a lot.

Sometimes I would confess to God and then a week later, I would go back and do the same thing. I would feel guilty because I thought I was wasting God's time. But this is so untrue, God is willing and ready to give us the chance as long as we are willing to come to Him.

Don't turn away from God, don't run away from Him, He is the deliverer. The devil will make you think that going to God is pointless, and you may think that as well. He would plant seeds of hopelessness in your mind, he will recall your past and remind you how you've struggled with the addiction for years, and he would try to convince you that there is no way out. Don't listen to him, don't believe him. He is a liar. Rather keep praying and trusting God to help you out. Look at the life of Moses, he was tending to his sheep when he saw the burning bush. Moses was scared, to see a bush that was on fire but not consuming. Moses' curiosity trumped his fear, and he went closer.

The burning bush was God the 'I am. It was at this point that God revealed His plan of rescue to Moses. His plan was to set the Israelites free from slavery. Moses at the time doubted himself. Moses was basically implying that he didn't have the skill, in public speaking to tell Pharaoh, 'Let my people go'. As I read in GNB (Good News Bible) I started to realise that Moses wasn't confident in himself, he was scared. That's how we are with our addiction – you are going through a season of change, and this change isn't a change that is easy, but God promises healing and help.

God said to Moses, "Didn't I give you a tongue?" And one of

the wonderful things about this text is that I finally realised that God is right. You were whole before your addiction, therefore, you can be whole again.

I know it seems tough, and you feel like you can never come out of the cycle, but God is telling you today, that He has given you the tools to become whole, and you will be freed from your addiction. Patterns can be difficult to break, but they can be broken. There were times when I felt like I couldn't control my food addiction until I went to God and I remembered the answer He gave to Moses, "Didn't I give you a tongue?" So, when I feel like I can't stop. I asked God to help me. I asked Him to provide the healing that I need so desperately, and I don't run from it. I allow God to change me, step by step. These are some helpful verses from the Bible that helps. **Exodus 14: 13 says,**" And Moses said unto the people, Fear ye not, stand still, and see the salvation of the LORD, which he will shew to you today: for the Egyptians whom ye have seen today, ye shall see them again no more forever." **Psalm 46:10,** "Be still, and know that I am God: I will be exalted among the heathen, I will be exalted in the earth." **Isaiah chapter 30:7**; "For the Egyptians shall help in vain, and to no purpose: therefore, have I cried concerning this, Their strength is to sit still." God's word is truly wonderful.

God was so understanding of Moses's fear of public speaking that He came down and decided that He will employ, Aaron, Moses's brother. There's something powerful about that text. There's an Aaron for you and God can provide you an Aaron when you feel like you're at your lowest or you feel like you can't get through your addiction even with God in it. There have been times when I felt like I couldn't do it. I couldn't battle my desire to gamble and therefore I decided to walk away from God instead of asking Him to work through my addiction, by my side. God will put people in your life – these people will help you with accountability. When you are going through your addiction, you need accountability, you need someone to be by your side. You need someone to look after you holistically and you need a love element to be there. Because the road that you're going through is tough but it's worth it. It's worth every sweat, tear, and frustration because, in the end, you will get your life back. And it won't be like before, you won't fall back into patterns because you've got God by your side. God is going to do *anything*, and anything to make sure that you're okay.

God has made a promise to us that He will do the impossible. So, whatever doubts you may have, call unto God, and explain to Him, how He can help you and He will.

You are ready.

Are you ready to let God take over your situation? What is keeping you from wanting change? I mentioned 'you are ready because God is ready to change you. He wants to bring that mountain down not to make it into a hill but a flat plain. You might have that alcohol in your hand or that needle in your arms, but this is the time where you put it down and try the power of God.

You might not have heard of God's power before, but I assure you if you call on the name of Jesus, His power will be activated and made manifest. Try it. Say JESUS! He will come to your rescue. God loves you and will take care of you. Be not afraid.

Chapter Twenty-four

Where are you heading to?

The Bible talks about two pathways; one broad and one narrow. The Broadway is the path that leads to destruction while the narrow road is the assurance of eternal life. Before I could tell which, one seems right or is the right way to head to let's hear what the Bible says about them both.

The broad route is Expansive and Effortless to Follow.

Matthew 7:13-14 says, "Enter through the narrow gate. For wide is the gate and broad is the road that leads to destruction, and many enter through it. But small is the gate and narrow the road that leads to life, and only a few find it." The pathway to heaven as the Bible said is narrow in the sense that there are principles, rules, and laws for you to follow. Many people claim they love God, but their movement demonstrates that they really hate Him. This can be very sad because God desires for none to perish. His love for us is everlasting and unconditional love. God wants you to head in His direction when you decide to begin that walk. He has prepared a place more beautiful than our wildest imagination for us. When you decide to take that step and you feel like there is enough space in a broad way, it is easier to walk through. Yes, it may be so, but the Bible says it leads to destruction. Destruction can lead to ruin, and ruin can cost us an opportunity for God's unfailing love. The broad and easy way can be followed without thought. It's spacious to walk on, and there are so many attractive things of the world to tempt and seduce our minds the fast car, the bling the mansions the fast life as some say, the Broadway is of the unreflective it is all about self and not of God. It is more carnally minded. God doesn't want us to fall prey to this kind of journey He knows that is the devil's way of tempting us to lose our eternal life. The devil himself and his wicked angels are doomed for hell. The saying goes misery wants company, don't be that company to walk in that broad way, life is not certain on Broadway to stay in the lane that leads to your Heavenly father. Take God at His word He will help you with the walk and sustain you with His strength, it is perfect and real. The world's views on God are not welcoming and true. As you can see the world doesn't like to adhere to the principles of God. God created this world centred on his principles. When these are rejected or denied, it can have detrimental effects, pain, hurt and sadness, and sometimes death. When we walk the Broadway again it will lead us to the plans that God never set for us. We want to stay on the path that is not carnally minded. "For to be carnally minded is death, but to be spiritually minded is life and peace Romans 8:6."

Chapter Twenty-five

The narrow path may seems
difficult but step on

Just imagine walking on the straight narrow road where not many on that road this can become a lonely road. The narrow road it is a path that illustrates the principles that God laid out for us to follow in other to have a sound relationship with Him and to have eternal life. There are many people who don't desire this life because they find it difficult for many reasons, for them serving God requires discipline comment and not everyone wants to be that way. For some people, the constant battle with sin and the fight against their mind's thoughts can drain them to the brink of letting go. God knows it is difficult for many people, He knows that we will always battle with sin. But He reminds us of being still and knows that the battles are not ours, but He will combat our conflicts for us. Don't try to quit and prepare to walk on the broad road. You will get tied you will get lost it is not straight you will become confused there are all kinds of disturbances that will ruin your love and the relationship you have with Him.

Following God is the way that will lead to a perfect life, we need to embrace the opportunity and determine in our heart to mustard the strength to walk with God. God calls us to be perfect as He is perfect. His purpose for us is to help us conquer sin. Matthew 7:1-6, Christ calls for His disciples to help others to take the specks or splinters out of their eyes. His aim is to save us and deliver mankind from sin. The narrow path for many can be difficult for the trials and even persecution they might experience.

   In the last beatitude, Jesus said that you will be persecuted because of righteousness (Matt 5:10). You will be persecuted because of your belief in the principle of God. People who choose to walk on Broadway dislike any limitations that thwart their comfort. To tell or even teach someone that God's word is the truth will not always sit well with some people. Many mock you when you are walking on the narrow road sometimes, they will say you have a boring life. In the book of second Timothy three and verses, twelve "for those who want to live Christlike life will be persecuted." Likewise, Paul again mentioned Galatians 2:20, *I have been crucified with Christ and I no longer live, but Christ lives in me."* In order to stay on the narrow way, you must give up the things that will hinder you from finding God's truth and move from the enslavement of sin to those that may have the potential to corrupt your thinking and silence your belief in God. Jesus said if anyone wants to walk with me or prepare to take the walk with Him, they must forsake everything and anyone that prepare to discourage them from coming to him. In Luke 14:26, Christ said that "if anyone wants to follow him, he must hate his father, mother, brother, sister, and even his own life to be his disciple." Luke here is encouraging that will need to give away our hearts to God willing. God desire for us to live an eternal and meaningful and fruitful life with him. Sometimes following God many times separates you from the people you love. But the reality here is that his desire is to save you, us. The narrow way calls for you and me to give up the things of the world. The Bible says the things of the world will deem and lose their values.

The Narrow Pathway can be difficult, but it leads to life.

Even the narrow way can be difficult, this route leads to life. Entering this path is a new experience to new life. Narrow path is the eternal path to life, and it is the path where you will find God. Many will ridicule you on the path because for them this path has no excitement. no thrill that is a big lie from the devil because he want you to keep away from God tender loving care. Though you may encountered trials and tribulation and be mocked by your belief in God but there is can be calmness in the midst of what you will go through a greater quality of life because of familiarity with God. When we walk the Lord God, it is a beauty in holiness so I encourage you to trust in Him, and He will show His greatness. Come to God all he that heavy laden he will give you rest peace while you in the narrow road. In Matthew 11:28-30 "Come to me, all you who are weary and burdened, and I will give you rest. Take my yoke on you and learn from me, because I am gentle and humble in heart, and you will find rest for your souls. For my yoke is easy to bear, and my load is not hard to carry." For those who choose to walk in the narrow pathway in Matthew chapter 5, gives such a wonderful insight it is what God says let the Bible talk.

"And seeing the multitudes, he went up into a mountain: and when he was set, his disciples came unto him: And he opened his mouth, and taught them, saying, Blessed are the poor in spirit: for theirs is the kingdom of heaven. Blessed are they that mourn for they shall be comforted. Blessed are the meek: for they shall inherit the earth. Blessed are they which do hunger and thirst after righteousness: for they shall be filled. Blessed are the merciful: for they shall obtain mercy. Blessed are the pure in heart: for they shall see God. Blessed are the peacemakers: for they shall be called the children of God. Blessed are they which are persecuted for righteousness sake: for theirs is the kingdom of heaven. Blessed are ye, when men shall revile you, and persecute you, and shall say all manner of evil against you falsely, for my sake. Rejoice, and be exceeding glad: for great is your reward in heaven: for so persecuted they the prophets which were before you. Ye are the salt of the earth: but if the salt has lost his savour, wherewith shall it be salted? it is thenceforth good for nothing, but to be cast out, and to be trodden under foot of men. Ye are the light of the world. A city that is set on a hill cannot be hidden. Neither do men light a candle, and put it under a bushel, but on a candlestick; and it giveth light unto all that are in the house. Let your light so shine before men, that they may see your good works, and glorify your Father which is in heaven. Think not that I am come to destroy the law or the prophets: I am not come to destroy, but to fulfil. For verily I say unto you, Till heaven and earth pass, one jot or one tittle shall in no wise pass from the law, till all be fulfilled. Whosoever, therefore, shall break one of these least commandments, and shall teach men so, he shall be called the least in the kingdom of heaven: but whosoever shall do and teach them, the same shall be called great in the kingdom of heaven. For I say unto you, That except your righteousness shall exceed the righteousness of the scribes and Pharisees, ye shall in no case enter into the kingdom of heaven. Ye have heard that it was said of them of old time, Thou shalt not kill, and whosoever shall kill shall be in danger of the judgment: But I say unto you, That whosoever is angry with his brother without a cause shall be in danger of the judgment: and whosoever shall say to his brother, Raca, shall be in danger of the council: but whosoever shall say, Thou fool, shall be in danger of hell fire. Therefore, if thou bring thy gift to the altar, and there remembers that thy brother hath ought against thee; Leave there thy gift before the altar and go thy way; first be reconciled to thy brother, and then come and offer thy gift. Agree with thine adversary quickly, whiles thou art in the way with him; lest at any time the adversary deliver thee to the judge, and the judge deliver thee to the officer, and thou be cast into prison.

Verily I say unto thee, Thou shalt by no means come out thence, till thou hast paid the uttermost farthing. Ye have heard that it was said by them of old time, Thou shalt not commit adultery: But I say unto you, That whosoever looked on a woman to lust after her hath committed adultery with her already in his heart. And if thy right eye offends thee, pluck it out, and cast it from thee: for it is profitable for thee that one of thy members should perish, and not that thy whole body should be cast into hell. And if thy right hand offend thee, cut it off, and cast it from thee: for it is profitable for thee that one of thy members should perish, and not that thy whole body should be cast into hell. It hath been said, Whosoever shall put away his wife, let him give her writing of divorcement: But I say unto you, That whosoever shall put away his wife, saving for the cause of fornication, caused her to commit adultery: and whosoever shall marry her that is divorced committed adultery. Again, ye have heard that it hath been said by them of old time, Thou shalt not forswear thyself, but shalt perform unto the Lord thine oaths: But I say unto you, Swear not at all; neither by heaven; for it is God's throne: Nor by the earth; for it is his footstool: neither by Jerusalem; for it is the city of the great King. Neither shalt thou swears by thy head, because thou canst not make one hair white or black. But let your communication be, Yea, yea; Nay, nay: for whatsoever is more than this cometh of evil.

Ye have heard that it hath been said, An eye for an eye, and a tooth for a tooth:

But I say unto you, That ye resist not evil: but whosoever shall smite thee on thy right cheek, turn to him the other also. And if any man will sue thee at the law, and take away thy coat, let him have thy cloak also. And whosoever shall compel thee to go a mile, go with him twain. Give to him that asked thee, and from him, that would borrow of thee turn not thou away. Ye have heard that it hath been said, Thou shalt love thy neighbour, and hate thine enemy. But I say unto you, Love your enemies, bless them that curse you, do good to them that hate you, and pray for them which despitefully use you, and persecute you; That ye may be the children of your Father which is in heaven: for He maketh His sun to rise on the evil and on the good, and sendeth rain on the just and on the unjust. For if ye love them which love you, what reward have ye? do not even the publicans the same? And if ye salute your brethren only, what do ye more than others? do not even the publicans so? Be ye therefore perfect, even as your Father which is in heaven is perfect."

Matthew chapter 5 Jesus has clearly spoken his heart to us he wants us to transform into good citizens so that the world can see him in us. The world can see who Jesus is in our eyes as so to desire to follow him. As mentioned, it will be difficult walking on the pathway that leads to life, but the honest truth keeps on walking when choose to walk it need to be the walk that will lead to life eternal. Remember the devil is like a roaring lion seeking to devour especially those that are vulnerable and those that have decided in making their wrongs right.

Chapter Twenty-six

Humble yourself before God.

Humbling yourself before God is a form of surrendering to God demonstrating that when you choose to walk with God you want Him to help direct you and give you the gears to walk. It is showing God that you cannot do it on your own, you are powerless, you need His intervention.

"Humble yourselves, therefore, under God's mighty hand, that He may lift you up in due time. Cast all your anxiety on Him because He cares for you. Be alert and of a sober mind. Your enemy the devil prowls around like a roaring lion looking for someone to devour. Resist him, standing firm in the faith, because you know that the family of believers throughout the world is undergoing the same kind of suffering. And the God of all grace, who called you to His eternal glory in Christ, after you have suffered a little while, Himself will restore you and make you strong, steady, and steadfast. To Him be the power forever and ever. Amen."

How can we enter the kingdom of heaven?

The answer is we can only enter the kingdom of God through Christ Jesus. He has paid the price in order so that we can gain eternal life and have it abundantly. All because God wants and desires are for all to come to know Him as their personal saviour. John 3: 16-17 tells the wonderful goodness of God. "For God so loved the world that he gave his one and only Son, that whoever believes in Him shall not perish but have eternal life. For God did not send his Son into the world to condemn the world, but to save the world through Him". God wants you and me and everyone in Heaven who believe in Him. Sometimes people feel like they don't want to come to know God because of fear that their deeds will be exposed or feel that God will hold them responsible, and will not forgive them. This is simply not true God is not here to denounce but His purpose is to save whosoever willingly comes to Him through Jesus Christ. I remember when I decided to give my life to God at first, I thought I would be missing out on things. I thought holding onto things of the world back then would make me happy. Going to the club or disco parties I thought that was happiness to me. But when I did go, I would always come into confrontations because if I did not choose to dance with a person, they often times pick on me swear at me, or simply cause a fuss. I thought again getting to know God would be boring and that He was going to govern my life. Despite all this way of thinking I decided I am going to give God a chance in my life. As soon as I made the baby steps to God, I find those steps to feel beautiful and wonderful so I decided to take bigger steps and today I can see the splendours of God's wonderful affection for me, my children, my husband, and all those around me. Sometimes in life you may feel like serving God is not something that you want to take on right now because you feel like you are too young, you just started life you want to see the world and experience the world. And you feel like you will be denied of your choice for you it will be governed. God never forces He never compels He is a redeemer a saviour, saving sinners from their sins. Yes, it may seem the pleasures of the world is sweet yes I use to think so as well as getting all dancing my heart out drinking beers, and just having a hangover the next day. This was simply killing me softly. Thank the Lord He brought me back to His reality. I am happy God helped me. God wants to bring us to safety. There are people who have abided by the things of the world, and they have not come back happy they have been distracted by the use of drugs, alcohol sex, and many perplexities of life have ruined them. It is a sad thing to comprehend. But this is what happens when we choose broadways of life. We must try to head in the right direction that leads to the remarkable light which is found in the word of God. God's word is like a lamp unto our feet and a light unto our path.

Jesus Teaches Nicodemus about the kingdom of heaven.

"Now there was a Pharisee, a man named Nicodemus who was a

member of the Jewish ruling council. ² He came to Jesus at night and said, "Rabbi, we know that you are a teacher who has come from God. For no one could perform the signs you are doing if God were not with him." Jesus replied, Very truly I tell you, no one can see the kingdom of God unless they are born again."

"How can someone be born when they are old?" Nicodemus asked. "Surely they cannot enter a second time into their mother's womb to be born!"

Jesus answered, Very truly I tell you, no one can enter the kingdom of God unless they are born of water and the Spirit. Flesh gives birth to flesh, but the Spirit gives birth to spirit. You should not be surprised at my saying, 'You must be born again. The wind blows wherever it pleases. You hear its sound, but you cannot tell where it comes from or where it is going. So, it is with everyone born of the Spirit. How can this be? Nicodemus asked. You are Israel's teacher," said Jesus, "and do you not understand these things? Very truly I tell you, we speak of what we know, and we testify to what we have seen, but still, you people do not accept our testimony. I have spoken to you of earthly things, and you do not believe; how then will you believe if I speak of heavenly things? No one has ever gone into heaven except the one who came from heaven—the Son of Man. Just as Moses lifted up the snake in the wilderness, so the Son of Man must be lifted up, that everyone who believes may have eternal life in Hi

Chapter Twenty-seven

Building your strength with God

Sometimes it can seems hard to build your strength in God when you have come from a place that has broken your spirit your way of thinking. Sometimes it could be in a business where you lost all your money or someone you love so dearly. It could be in a relationship where your trust was betrayed and in places where you felt disrespected and so lost and empty. You are in that mind-set you don't want to try anything else because you don't want to play the waiting game anymore. This is painful it is scary, but the good news is that there is hope when you fall, it is not as simple but there is a God above that can accommodate where you are in your life. He has experience in mending the broken-hearted and setting the captive free. He will take you to a next level where those who you cannot hurt you no more.. Be strong and let's pray! As I do so I want you to say nothing and just allow the peace of God to do the talking.

Prayer

Father God, I come to you in Jesus' name in good faith that the one who said this prayer can feel your peace, it is very hard for anyone who has encountered some form of brokenness, it is not easy for them to get up and dust themselves and say it okay and move on and walk about like a walk in the park. No father it is not easy it is difficult for them.

Please father God give them your strength so that they can be able to walk again in true gladness. Show them the way which is the narrow path to walk in. Help them with their unbelief and teach them to love again in Jesus' name. Amen.

This prayer is an indication that when you pray God will answer you. I encourage you today to start praying to God and He will answer you. God will clean you up and give you a clean slate of life. God is a true builder. Building your strength in Him will bring you to a place where you will be able to overcome anything and everything. I remember I used to be a chicken not literally, I said chicken because I was worrying a lot then about any and everything. I used to think that God's timing was taking too long so I wanted to do it my way searching or pursuing in my own strength. WRONG! Oh, how silly I was to think that. It never work I was still in the same place of worry. Some of my worries were *"what if or maybe? Should and would and could."* These words diminish my way of thinking and delay my progress. Until that day when I try Jesus and seek to have His strength, my thinking began to feel different. As a matter-of-fact God's help was quicker than I thought. It took me 5 years trying in my own strength and I never achieved anything. With the strength of God, it took weeks for God to transform me. From that very moment, I felt a breath of spiritual fresh air. Amazing and wonderful. The way I went on to build my strength in God was first, I surrendered to God by just acknowledging who He was and inviting Him into my life I began to pray and spend time in His words in the Bible. The more I spend time with God the less worried I became. I started loving that feeling it felt so GOOD! I said to myself "I am not letting go of God." I understood the trust I was building in God was real and true. God was changing me to His perfection, and this is a beautiful feeling. I was tasting the Goodness of God and still is. As King David said, "taste and see that the Lord God is good," He truly is good. Please try Him for yourself and have that wonderful experience with the Lord God almighty. Yeah! It is a **Beautiful** and **Awesome** feeling.

Chapter Twenty-eight

Recover, Retract, Relive; live your life in peace

I want to tell you that once you've decide to follow God there will be some trials that will come your way to stop you, because the devil plans is to stop you from finding out for yourself who God is. He don't wants you to experience the blessing that God have for you. Imagine when the devil was with God, he was highly favoured he could sing in all the notes he was beautiful, and he still can sing and is still beautiful the only thing is he undeniably wicked. He and his awful angels are the obstacles that so desire to stand in the way of your blessings from God.

For those of you who are new in searching for God, you might think why God allowed the enemy to be in this world to cause disturbance. The thing is God doesn't react in anger. He does not use violence to change things.

One day when He comes back for His world those of us that chose to be part of God's mission will be able to Judge Satan and his angels and those who choose to love the world instead of God.

The subtitle here is **Recover**; try and allow the Holy Spirit to recover you from the stronghold that pulls you down, try or walk into his goodness walk to the path that will enhance you to purity and contentment.

Retract; find the need to apologise for the things that you have done wrong God is not here to condemn you but to save you. He wants to give you the opportunity for you to have a relationship with Him. God's plan is to have His children live forever. Why not it is beautiful and will be beautiful when we all make it to heaven. It will be the most beautiful feeling.

Relive; remember God's plans are certain for they shall come to pass. Don't be fooled by the world's way of showing you how to live and that you matter and not God.

Be sober and vigilant the world is there to distract you from finding the one true God. where are you heading, walking in God's direction is important. So, walk into God's great light and live the life of peace that He has promised to give you. It is a peace that permits all understanding.

Jesus wants you to follow Him.

The narrow path as you know leads to the path to eternity a path that Jesus walk as an example, in order to have total commitment with God. Jesus wants you to be committed to God to take up your cross and follow Him while it is time. Don't delay He is pleading.

In mark 8:34-38

Then He called the crowd to Him along with his disciples and said: "Whoever wants to be my disciple must deny themselves and take up their cross and follow me. For whoever wants to save their life will lose it, but whoever loses their life for me and for the gospel will save it. What good is it for someone to gain the whole world, yet forfeit their soul? Or what can anyone give in exchange for their soul? If anyone is ashamed of me and my words in this adulterous and sinful generation, the Son of Man will be ashamed of them when he comes in his Father's glory with the holy angels."

Completely, in your walk let it be a walk on the narrow pathway.

John 14: 15 (GNB) says "If you love me, you will obey my commandments."

Amos 5:15 (GNB) says "Hate what is evil, love what is right, and see that justice prevails in the courts. Perhaps the LORD will be merciful to the people of this nation who are still left alive." **Leviticus 19:18** (GNB) says "Do not take revenge on anyone or continue to hate him but love your neighbour as you love yourself. I am the LORD."

Chapter Twenty-nine

Vanity

Vanity as I remember as a child referred by my grandma as her sofa, indeed it was a beautiful sofa. She used to say, *"child sit on my vanity properly."* She adored that sofa so much. The story is not to talk of my grandma sofa she adored. But to share with you that vanity is not a nice thing to allow in your life it can be destructive, vanity can cause a person to become vain and empty. King Solomon talked about vanity it made him glorify his own self and not God, he said all that he adored was empty and vexation of the soul. The wealth and women he had did not satisfy him it made him feel empty meaning he was not happy at all because his show-off attitude offended God. His vanity caused him to bow down to false gods. Vanity was a stronghold, a mountain in Solomon's life. He could not break that mountain it takes God's intervention to renew the mind of Solomon back to the understanding of where he should be spiritually. Vanity is a stronghold it brings pride self-indulgence false sense of make believe a chain that needs to be broken. "Vanity of vanities, saith the Preacher, vanity of vanities; all is vanity," Ecclesiastes 1:2. You should not let the things of the world dominate your every move in life. God will help you ask him for his help. Vanity has led many people into a dark place, sadly for some it was a point of no return. Jezebel Ahab wife was full of vanity it never led to a good ending for her, the full story is in (**1 Kings 21:5–16**). Another example is King Saul a gifted and talented man allowed by God to be king. He let vanity get in his life and rule over him. Saul refused to humble himself before God but choose to be self-important and disregard the principles and commands of God. The end result for Saul God's spirit was no longer in him. *(read the book of 1 Samuel and further reading of King Saul.)* I want you to pause here and switch off your phone if you have to. Just imagine God's spirit is no longer in you, how would you feel? For me, I would be DAVASTATED! Oh God helps us. The thought of asking this question is painful. Let's pray.

Prayer

Dear Heavenly Father God in the name of Jesus we come before you. It is a need and desperation to come to you. The life that we live is uncertain. It is easy to be distracted and to get caught up by the things of the world, which can cause us to lose focus and fall short and miserable. Lord, please let not vanity and all other negatives persuade us to follow the models of Saul or anyone that dishonour you. The thought of not having your spirit in us is insane, may your spirit remain in us PERMANENTLY!

Thank you Lord God we pray in Jesus's name Amen.

Vanity and all other types of dark forces don't only affect you but can cause destress and heartbreak to families and even friends. When you adored material things you are setting up yourself for falls you will do things that you don't normally do to feed that lifestyle. There is are stories where people have compromised their trust and fall victim to vanity. It is a sad story to see the impact vanity could have on people. When they allowed their minds into ungodly things there will be consequences. Vanity denotes what is significant and brings out what is awful. The blessed news is that God is not there to outcast you nor is he there to turn His back on you. He doesn't want you to fall into Satan trap where Satan adored his own beauty and wanted to be god himself. God wants to free you so that you will be victorious in your walk of life. God is wonderful and amazing God. It is not too late for him to dismantle any forces of life that have trapped you. Give Him the green light right now and prove him. God will come through when you think that the exit is blocked. Look upon God the greatest of the great He is the freedom fighter that will roar your troubles away. You are not been put on this earth to be a victim of vanity if anything a victor of God's victory. From the stronghold of vanity. God wants us not to be lovers of things of the world because things of the world will deem and lose their value. Nothing in this world last forever, however, it is certain that God's love last forever.

Chapter Thirty

Hoarding

Hoarding! Wow, where do I start a big mountain that stands in the way of many individuals that fell victim to. It is like those crippling plant or a spider web that entangles around you. It is very sad and disturbing way to live life like a hoarder. The things is some people intentions was not be a hoarder. But there are trials and difficulties where people fell victim to such practices. Certain voids in your lives can bring on such behaviour. Divorce, losing a job, a child, and lots more can facilitate those behaviours. These things don't just start overnight but gradually hoarding creeps into your life and create havoc in your head. Some people may go through a divorce and the pressure of it can live a void in order to full fill that void they hold on to stuff that they don't need and accumulate other stuff that they don't need either. For example, that person may buy things they don't need but because they want to fill that void they will continue to buy and buy, and they just cannot stop. God is love He will help you. **Philippians 4:11-13:** "Not that I am speaking of being in need, for I have learned in whatever situation I am to be content. I know how to be brought low, and I know how to abound. In any and every circumstance, I have learned the secret of facing plenty and hunger, abundance, and need. I can do all things through him who strengthens me."**2 Corinthians 12:9-10:** "But he said to me, 'My grace is sufficient for you, for my power is made perfect in weakness.' Therefore, I will boast all the more gladly of my weaknesses, so that the power of Christ may rest upon me. For the sake of Christ, then, I am content with weaknesses, insults, hardships, persecutions, and calamities. For when I am weak, then I am strong." The Bible God's words have given you hope so in all your difficulties trust in God continually/

Stand Still Says (SSS) the Lord
2 Chronicles 32:8

"With him is an arm of flesh, but with us is the LORD our God to help us, and to fight our battles. And the people rested themselves upon the words of Hezekiah king of Judah."

These are some of the books in the Bible that tell us what God says about His power. Stand still and see His salvation. You need to sap into God's word and berry yourselves in there in order to have a full sense of where God is aiming for you. His objectives for you and others are perfect. The end goal for God is for you to spend eternity with Him. But you have to acknowledge there is power in the name of Jesus to break every chain, not one chain but every chain that is holding you down. Believe in the master plans for you. You are one of his masterpieces why not start to think that way then you can become that way because God wants you in that direction. Chains were not made to hold you down but for the devil and his wicked angels. Peace and joy and happiness are designed for a child of a King, and who is the King? He is King Jesus. The Man of Power. Power to **Break** every Chain. Starting with your chains, your addiction, and your mountain.

Chapter Thirty-one

If there is an Entrance, there should be an Exit

Where there is a beginning there must be an ending. If there is an entrance, there should be an exit. You must be wondering what I am trying to say. Well, the big picture is the chain will fall. The troubles you are experiencing as long as you give it to God He will help you go through it victoriously. Sometimes with some of the troubles, you are facing, you may ask yourself why you put yourself in such a situation that is beyond your control, be not dismayed, God will give you an exit. Meaning God will end it for you. God knows you very well He alone can break your chain, your fights, and the strongholds. Give God the opportunity to work in your life, He does an excellent job. The Bible talks about the woman with the issue of blood. For a very long, time, this woman in the Bible suffered from this condition, and no one ever took notice of her. How distressed she must have felt. She went to many doctors and maybe traditional doctors for a cure yet still none could help her. In those days when people were sick for long periods of time, people could be quick to say it was either a curse or God was punishing the sufferer for their sins. This woman must have felt hopeless and confused with that chain of infirmity in her life. I guess those who knew her must have wondered what sin the woman had committed to deserve such affliction.

A brief story of the woman

In Luke chapter 8 verses 43 to 48, there was a woman who had been subject to bleeding for twelve years, but no one could heal her. She came up behind Jesus and touched the edge of His cloak, and immediately her bleeding stopped. "Who touched me?" Jesus asked. When they all denied it, Peter said, "Master, the people are crowding and pressing against you." But Jesus said, "Someone touched me; I know that power has gone out from me."

Then the woman, seeing that she could not go unnoticed, came trembling and fell at his feet. In the presence of all the people, she told why she had touched him and how she had been instantly healed. Then he said to her, "Daughter, your faith has healed you. Go in peace."

The good news is that her breakthrough came when she came into connection with Jesus. Jesus was in town that day so the woman must have heard the news that Jesus was in town. She went looking for Jesus because she was determined to be free of her chains. Sometimes you have to have that determination and boldly take that step for Jesus to break your chain. When the woman got to the place where Jesus was, and she whispered to herself, "*if only I can touch him, I will be healed.*" She burst through that crowd and went straight for Jesus she was not able to touch Jesus, but she touched the hem of His garment, and that was enough for Jesus to say who touch me? The moment she touched Jesus, healing took place, and her chains came crashing down.

Hallelujah! She was set free. No more confusion, no more isolation, no more avoidance from people or being treated like a pariah, she was whole again! This is a wonderful story that demonstrates the power and greatness of God. Today, you might be thinking you have been through so much, gone to therapy, and tried all sources that were recommended to you, yet nothing has worked. You are like that woman who tried everything, and not anything work out. Where there is an Entrance there should be an Exit. When everything else failed the woman with the issue of blood, she decided to try Jesus. And immediately, her chains fell off. This is the power of God to change you. Another powerful and moving narrative is the story of a man named Jairus a church leader, who came to Jesus' feet, pleading to come to his house to heal his only daughter of twelve who had the chains of death she was dying. Imagine how this man was feeling, right then and there as his only daughter, was on the verge of passing away. Anyone who loses a daughter could feel depressed and hopeless in that situation.

Jairus, however, was ready to give Jesus permission to free his daughter from the death grip. Jesus break that chain of death from Jairus's daughter, and she was set free.

Chapter Thirty-two

Listening to the chains falling

There is a song by the lovely Tasha Cobbs that says, '*I hear the chains falling*'. Oh yes, there are strongholds and chains that need to be broken. Jesus desires that every soul should be saved. Jesus said, "Come to me all ye that are heavy laden, and I will give you rest." That rest is peace, that rest is your chains that will be broken you will feel the joy of the freedom that He will give you for life.

In Galatian5:1, Paul says "Christ has set us free; stand firm therefore, and do not submit again to a yoke of bondage." Addictions can keep you in the yoke of bondage, but Jesus is here to set you free from the chains that are stopping you from becoming whom God has created you to be. Nothing is more relieving than burdens being taken off your shoulders. Imagine your foot got stuck between rails, you've tried to push and twist but nothing seems to be helping. You bend over your foot, worried and anxious, not knowing what to do. Then someone stops by, and firmly but gently pulls out your foot. How do you feel? That's right, relief washes over you. It's the same way when you surrender your addiction to Jesus and ask Him to break the chains. Whatever the chain or stronghold might be, God wants to deliver you. Christ delivers anyone that chooses to come to Him. There is nothing under the heavens that is too strong for God to break down. God asked Jeremiah a question *"is there anything too hard for me?"* The answer God can make the impossible possible nothing is too hard for God He is God. The word of God says for our warfare not of the flesh but have divine power to destroy strongholds addictions. *2 Corinthians 3:17* stated "Now the Lord is the Spirit, and where the Spirit of the Lord is, there is freedom." And Ephesians 6:10-18 "Finally, be strong in the Lord and in the strength of his might. Put on the whole armour of God, that you may be able to stand against the schemes of the devil. For we do not wrestle against flesh and blood, but against the rulers, against the authorities, against the cosmic powers over this present darkness, against the spiritual forces of evil in the heavenly places. Therefore, take up the whole armour of God, that you may be able to withstand in the evil day, and having done all, to stand firm. Stand therefore, having fastened on the belt of truth, and having put on the breastplate of righteousness, in order to stand the fiery weapons of the devil." Remember, he cannot win any match as long as God's armour is upon you. **Nahum 1:7** "The Lord is good, a stronghold in the day of trouble; he knows those who take refuge in him. "Luke 10:19 "Behold, I have given you authority to tread on serpents and scorpions, and over all the power of the enemy, and nothing shall hurt you." *Galatian 5:1-26* "For freedom, Christ has set us free; stand firm therefore, and do not submit again to a yoke of slavery. Look: I, Paul, say to you that if you accept circumcision, Christ will be of no advantage to you. I testify again to every man who accepts circumcision that he is obligated to keep the whole law. You are severed from Christ, you who would be justified by the law; you have fallen away from grace. For through the Spirit, by faith, we ourselves eagerly wait for the hope of righteousness." *Psalms 9:9*"The Lord is a stronghold for the oppressed, a stronghold in times of trouble." Stay focused on God!

Jesus broke the chain of the man possessed by demons. (Mark 5:1-20)

"They sailed to the region of the Gerasene's, which is across the lake from Galilee. When Jesus stepped ashore, he was met by a demon-possessed man from the town. For a long time, this man had not worn clothes or lived in a house but had lived in the tombs. When he saw Jesus, he cried out and fell at his feet, shouting at the top of his voice, "What do you want with me, Jesus, Son of the MostHigh God? I beg you, don't torture me!" For Jesus had commanded the impure spirit to come out of the man. Many times, it had seized him, and though he was chained hand and foot and kept under guard, he had broken his chains and had been driven by the demon into solitary places.

"Jesus asked him, 'What is your name?"

"Legion," he replied because many demons had gone into him.

And they begged Jesus repeatedly not to order them to go into the Abyss.

"A large herd of pigs was feeding there on the hillside. The demons begged Jesus to let them go into the pigs, and he gave them permission. When the demons came out of the man, they went into the pigs, and the herd rushed down the steep bank into the lake and drowned. When those tending the pigs saw what had happened, they ran off and reported this in the town and countryside, and the people went out to see what had happened." There are countless breakthroughs that Jesus has done, and He has the power to do so for you and everyone. In this book, you may come across the phrase *"Jesus will break down the chains"* because He will.

Chapter Thirty-three

Hope

1 Peter 5:10 says "And after you have suffered a little while, the God of all grace, who has called you to His eternal glory in Christ, will Himself restore, confirm, strengthen, and establish you."

Though most of Paul's scriptures were dedicated to Christian living and ministry building, I want to remind you that God desires a relationship with you; it doesn't matter if you are a pastor or layman, He wants to be your best friend. Paul in Colossians 1:23 (ESV) identified, what hope is, "If indeed you continue in the faith, stable and steadfast, not shifting from the hope of the gospel that you heard, which has been proclaimed in all creation under heaven, and of which I, Paul, became a minister." One thing we should pick out is **'not shifting from the hope of the gospel** I don't know your level of spiritual growth; if you have connections to Christ, grew up in the church, or still deciding if you want to become a Christian, but Paul is encouraging you to have faith. Faith in the dictionary is described as having complete trust and confidence in something. Our hope comes with faith. They go hand in hand. Sometimes, we don't have hope because we don't have faith that God will help us through our addiction. That leads us to self-doubt and depression. With the little faith, you have right now, believe that God is going to do it, He will change your life for the better, and your addiction will never be part of your life again. Believe it.

You also need to recognise that God can grow your faith. You might think, *no way He can't, but He can.* Christ tells us in Matthew 17: 20 (GNB) that we just need faith as big as a mustard seed. I want you to imagine a small, tiny grain, a tiny circle. A mustard seed is smaller than the tip of your finger and yet Christ says I assure you that if you have faith as big as a mustard seed, you can say to this hill, 'Go from here to there!' and it will go. You could do anything!" If we have that size of faith we can move mountains and do wonders in His name. All you need to do is to believe. It is awesome, how Jesus describes it. The description of the mustard seed made me think, how can that small amount of faith work? But it does work. Even if we have the tiniest piece of faith, God can work with that. Paul says to have faith that's " steadfast", steadfast means to be firm or immovable. That's how you need to treat your faith, Faith that no matter how many times you fall for your addiction, that you will get up. Have faith don't quit when you fail but get back up God can help you change.

He's your hope. God can be trusted. Jeremiah 17:7 says, "Blessed is the man who trusts in the LORD, and whose hope is the LORD." **Lamentation 3:24** "The LORD is my portion, says my soul, therefore I hope in Him!" **Zephaniah 3:17**"The LORD your God is in your midst, the Mighty One, will save; He will rejoice over you with gladness, He will quiet you with His love, He will rejoice over you with singing." **Romans 5:5** "Now hope does not disappoint, because the love of God has been poured out in our hearts by the Holy Spirit [which] was given to us." *Romans 15:4* "For whatever things were written before were written for our learning, that we through the patience and comfort of the Scriptures might have hope." **Romans 15:13** "Now may the God of hope fill you with all joy and peace in believing, that you may abound in hope by the power of the Holy Spirit."

When you are weak God is your strength. His strength is perfect. God is the one that is able to carry you through your journey. He knows exactly where to take you. All you have to do is trust Him. And again, never lean on your own understanding but on God's own understanding.

Chapter Thirty-four

Abandonment

Abandonment is one of the leading causes of trauma and heartache. Most people who have experienced abandonment usually feel depressed and react by isolating themselves from others, especially if they were abandoned by those they thought would always be there for them. Some people even refuse to speak of abandonment because they are ashamed of the sting of rejection.

These "coping measures" are understandable but not advisable. I understand bearing pain is difficult let alone talking about it. But you will feel better if you talk to someone who is ready to listen and able to help you. For those who are trapped by the trauma of abandonment, and are unable to move on, there is help for you. God has not forgotten about you. God will mend your broken heart and set you free.

Abandonment is like a vacuum, it sucks away one's energy. It is a frightening experience. People who have experienced abandonment as children normally see the effect in their adult life. However, with the help of God and therapy, they can have the will and motivation to live life to the fullest, free from shame and trauma. "The ear of the Lord is attuned to those who have been abandoned, and He is ever ready to help them and wipe away their tears. "The Lord is near to the broken-hearted and saves the crushed in spirit (Psalms 34: 18)". Abandonment is another chain God can break, all you have to do is give Him the opportunity to work on you. Seek the Lord, call on Him and He will deliver you from your fears. Those who look to Him are radiant, and will never be ashamed. God is not here to criticize you He is there to surround you with His love and angels to encamp around Psalms 91:12 says "For he will order his angels to protect you wherever you go. They will hold you up with their hands you won't even hurt your foot on a stone". Psalms 34:7 " the angel of the Lord God encamps around those who fear Him and delivers them."

Joseph and his many coloured coats (Genesis 37)

When we talk about abandonment in the Bible the first person that comes to mind is Joseph. When he was betrayed by his family and in most cases, this is how abandonment happens most people become traumatised and feel abundant because a family member may be their mother brother sister father left them. The second scenario is the point where Joseph must have felt abandoned by God this is most likely the point when he was walking under the scorching heat of the desert and being led away as a slave there must be confusion in in his head first from the betrayal of his brothers and then the confusion that comes when he started wondering why he was experiencing a horrible situation. Reading Joseph's story brought to light in an area of your life where you felt abandoned. Like Joseph God will help you.

In the end Joseph became a man with recognition the man second to next to King Pharoah.

Throughout Genesis 38, we understand what Joseph was going through. He experienced a difficult time as a slave, but Potiphar sees his diligence and rewards him for it. I call this period the "time of relaxation", it's a period in our lives where we have a bad situation, and we think it's fixed. For example, let's say, your father has abandoned you but 6 years later he comes back into your life. You feel the relaxation, you feel loved and you're happy that you're no longer abandoned.

But then there's a year of trouble. This happened to Joseph, he had a lovely relationship with Potiphar, however, Potiphar's wife began lusting after him. When her advancements were rejected, she lied against Joseph.. This is what I call the 'year of trouble' and it doesn't necessarily mean that it's an exact year, it could be a few years. Just like Joseph, he had to spend years in jail for a crime he didn't commit. During these times, abandonment stings, and it hurts. When a person is abandoned, they are likely to lose confidence, and they make poor choices because they believe that they deserve less. All because the person who abandoned you has left your life again. You thought they would show you the love you deeply desire but you receive the exact opposite. Unfortunately, the relationship hasn't changed and the person who has abandoned you has told you, it wouldn't change. This period was the darkest for Joseph, and I can imagine how it is for you.

But with every darkness, there is always a light. Joseph found that light when he was asked by two fellow prisoners to interpret their dream. He did. Later on, when one of the prisoners was released, he told the prisoner to remember him and to tell the King about him whenever he could. Years passed by but things didn't change.

At this stage, it was a struggle for Joseph waiting to hear a word of hope. It's a time when we reach out, we tell our friends, our family, a pastor, or a therapist about our problems but we still don't feel fulfilled. Sometimes in other ways, we call out for help, maybe you talk to your youngest sibling or half-sibling whom your parent likes more than you. Your parents may have expressed it, or they may not but you can tell they prefer the other sibling to you because they have a better relationship with them. They have a loving relationship, they've never seen that side of abandonment that you've experienced and so it's hard for you to speak your realities about that person because someone else has a positive experience with them. Abandonment looms over your head and during this time you're sad and not always hopeful as before.

However, just like things changed for Joseph when he was asked by the King to interpret his dream. There will be a moment in your life when God takes all of your pain, and He makes it into an opportunity for growth. The pain that you experience is suddenly washed away through a series of happy moments. You find a few families whether it be through friends or new or extended family. You find a loving partner or a business or cause which will allow you to help those who feel the way you felt. This stage is what I call the 'series of God's goodness ', at first you don't realise what happens but once you receive goodness, your trials feel like it was years ago.

If you would like to experience the phase of goodness overflow, you must allow God into your life. Allow Him to take control of your darkness and allow Him to show you the light.

God can provide us with something that we desire during abandonment - love. He replaces abandonment with love because that's who He is. Through the dark phases of my life, I have got to know God and trust Him. I have realised that I can never find a love so sweet as God. In 2 Peter 1:3 (NIV), it states, "His divine power has given us everything we need for a godly life through our knowledge of Him who called us by his own glory and goodness." This teaches me that God can give us many gifts, He can heal our hearts from abandonment, and He can provide the love that we need.

Deuteronomy 31: 6 says, "Be strong and courageous. Do not fear or be in dread of them, for it is the Lord your God who goes with you. He will not leave you or forsake you." When you feel abandoned or weak, God isn't asking you to be strong by becoming macho. He is asking you to draw closer to Him and tap from His well of strength. He means you should read the Bible, study His word, and realize that He will always be with you. He's not fake and neither is His love. He will help when you least expect it. He will give you strength. In addition, "Be strong and courageous" means be strong and face your abandonment head-on, don't allow it to take over your life, ruin your relationship with good people or make you think that you're not worthy. It takes courage to head through the cause of your abandonment and allow God to heal you from the trauma.

Don't let abandonment eat you alive, instead hold your head up and walk through it with God by your side, He is always with you and ready to walk to the ends of the Earth with you.

The moment you take to walk with God, rest assured that He will work through your fears. Sometimes we don't want to work through our abandonment issues because we are fearful. We are scared and feel undeserving of love. When fear seems to grab a hold of you, hold fast to Psalm 34:4, "I sought the Lord, and he answered me and delivered me from all my fears." God will help you through your fears, and you can beat the sad thoughts and the feeling of not being wanted or loved. God's plan for you is good and not evil. His desire is that you should prosper and be in good health, He loved you so dearly that He sent His only begotten son as a ransom for your sins. He wants your life to be beautiful and He is ready to supply all your needs (Philippians 4:19).

Chapter Thirty-five

He knows and hear you when you call

I tell everyone I meet that God is a generous giver who never gets tired of giving good gifts. His love is steadfast and unshakeable. It doesn't matter where you've been or what you've done, He still loves you. He has seen the mess you made and still calls you His own. He saw when you cheated on your partner, but still forgave you. He saw you when you were kicked out of your house, He saw when you decided to hide your pain and shame with drugs, and He saw when that person took advantage of you. He knows you and your broken parts and wants to comfort you, He wants to heal you and give you reasons to smile again. You don't have to walk on eggshells around Him, He knows you. Come to Him today. Talk to Him, cry to Him, and He will wrap you in His arms. . There were times when I was physically shouting at God, but it strengthened our relationship because even though I shouted my frustrations, I asked God to give me scriptures and place people in my life who can help me. I opened my heart and God gave me more – not money but skills, love, and a promise. A promise that He will always be there for me.(Micah 5:4, Isaiah 46:4, Isaiah 41:13, and Deuteronomy 1:31).

This is a beautiful text of encouragement.

1 Corinthians 15:10 NIV (NIV) says "But by the grace of God I am what I am, and his grace to me was not without effect. No, I worked harder than all of them--yet not I, but the grace of God that was with me."

The hard work that you need to do is to trust God, and once you do the hard work which is trusting in God and having faith in Him, work no longer feels hard – it feels rewarding. You will reap the benefits and if you don't believe it, please, read the passage again. God is ever ready to listen to you, He never likes to see you weary or broken-hearted God wants to heal your brokenness He feels your pain God is your friend. You may think that He is far but from a distance, God is watching over you. *"The songwriter says from a distance God is watching "*. That is true God will take care of you and will pick you up when you stumble and even when you fall.

You might think you've gone through so much, done too much, and God can never come through for you. I am here to tell you that is a lie from the pit of hell. There is no length God cannot go for you. He leaves the ninety-nine to find the one stray sheep. He will find you, but you must first surrender to Him. You must give Him space in your life. The fact that you are even alive to talk about your hard times is proof that God was with you all along.

He never abandoned you. Things will turn around for your good, and things will get better, but first, you must come to Him. And He will fight your battles, only be still and put your trust in Him.

This is where you write those addictions that are holding you down and making you feel awful. Write them, you are a conqueror in Jesus' name. Amen.

_____

_____

_____

_____

_____

_____

_____

_____

_____

_____

_____

_____

_____

_____

_____

_____

_____

_____

_____

_____

_____

This is where you affirm your way to positivity. Write down your affirmations with the letter your name begins with.

A

_____

_____

_____

_____

_____

_____

_____

_____

_____

_____

_____

B

_____

_____

_____

_____

_____

_____

_____

C

D

E

F

G

H

I

J

K

L

M

N

O

P

Q

R

S

T

U

V

W

X

Y

Z

Whatever month your Birthday falls I encourage you to write something Beautiful about yourself because you are Beautiful.

January

February

March

April

May

_____

_____

_____

_____

_____

_____

_____

_____

_____

_____

_____

_____

_____

_____

_____

_____

_____

_____

_____

_____

_____

_____

June

July

_____
_____
_____
_____
_____
_____
_____
_____
_____
_____
_____
_____
_____
_____
_____
_____
_____
_____
_____
_____
_____
_____
_____
_____

August

_____
_____
_____
_____
_____
_____
_____
_____
_____
_____
_____
_____
_____
_____
_____
_____
_____
_____
_____
_____
_____
_____
_____

September

October

November

December

Notes

Notes

Notes

Big thanks to everyone

Big thanks to everyone who took the time to read this book. I hope and Pray that the encouragement you have received in this book will help you on your journey to become a victor over your situation. I dare you to give God your addiction, and your mountain, and He will set you free.

Printed in Great Britain
by Amazon